Christian Principles: Raising the Bar

Engaging Lessons from the Sermon on the Mount

By
Steven A. Carlson

GUARDIAN
PUBLISHING, LLC

This edition published in July 2018 in association with

Guardian Publishing, LLC
Holt, Michigan

guardianpublishingllc.com

Acknowledgements

In the more than twenty-five years that I have served as a church elder, I have worked with various ministers of the gospel. I would like to dedicate this work to three ministers who have helped to shape my eldership as well as my writing and teaching during that time. Each has served as minister in my local congregation.

The first minister I would like to mention is Gregory Steere. His keen biblical insights and profound mastery of the English language affected me greatly. He was most influential in helping me learn to articulate my thoughts in a manner that, I believe, has allowed me to become a more effective teacher over the years.

The second minister who deserves credit is Dan Cameron. Being engrossed in Bible study and writing, as I often am, it is easy to miss the clues that tell you when someone is in need. When people are at their lowest, they need church family the most. Dan was always the first one to the hospital or to someone's home when they needed visitation and support. With Dan's help, I have learned to keep a watchful eye open for those in need.

The third minister is Conrad Gonzales. Conrad has helped me apply my understanding of Scripture to the body of Christ (the church) in a way that honors God. He has stressed the fact that church is family but also understands that it is a family that must be focused on the work of God. This has been invaluable to me. Spending time studying Scripture means nothing if the lessons learned are not applied in a manner that accomplishes what God intends.

This book is dedicated to these men and the work they have done for the kingdom over the years. Their friendship and the example each has provided have meant more to me than they could possibly know.

I would like to thank my sister, Naomi Nash, Craig Gates, who is a missionary and friend, and Mary Shutt, a schoolteacher and sister in Christ, for their proofreading/editing efforts. I could not have done it without them. Also, my wife, Denise, deserves recognition for being the most patient and supportive woman in the world. Only those who love to write can understand what that kind of support means to an aspiring author.

Preface

Here unfolds the basic principles of Christianity. The fifth through the seventh chapters of Matthew's gospel offer what is commonly called the *Sermon on the Mount*. This sermon constitutes one of the most popular and yet most controversial passages in all of Scripture. In general, Jesus deals with what should be the attitude of the believer along with some insight into more specific issues like murder, divorce, revenge, etc. The apostles continually repeat these numerous principles in the epistles that make up much of the New Testament.

Perhaps the most important point of this sermon is that, for the coming covenant of grace, Jesus seems to be raising the bar for those who wish to honor God. In the Old Testament, the Israelites honored God by obeying the Mosaic Law. Yet, it was always God's desire to have a graceful, spiritual relationship with men. In order for that to happen, the price for sin had to be paid. That is the very reason Jesus came to earth. Once that price was paid, mankind's relationship with God could be truly elevated to the spiritual plane God had in view. Jesus' words in this sermon are intended to provide guidelines for those who seek to live the kind of spiritual life God had always wanted for humankind.

It is unknown how long Jesus spoke. Perhaps Matthew has provided only some highlights from the sermon that he believed revealed the finer points of godliness. In its fullness, the sermon may have been much more comprehensive. John states that, had all Jesus said and done while on earth been recorded, "…even the world itself would not contain the books that would be written" (John 21: 25). Therefore, it could be that Matthew recorded only a synopsis of the sermon, highlighting those teachings deemed most important.

Some of the details found in Matthew's account also lend credence to the likelihood that the original sermon, as spoken by Jesus, encompassed much more than the apostle documented. This probability is generally agreed upon by bible scholars, many of whom tend to accept the proposition that the account Matthew has provided is abbreviated. Given the fact that people had traveled long distances to hear what Jesus had to say, it is unlikely that his discourse lasted a mere twenty minutes, which is roughly the length of time needed to read the Matthew account. According to D. A. Carson:

> ...by the end of his sermon (7: 28-29), he was surrounded by yet larger crowds. This suggests that his teaching covered several days, not just an hour or two...[1]

Jesus' words in this sermon provide better insight into how God thinks than had been previously offered. In a single discourse, he turned theological and doctrinal philosophy on its ear. People would no longer relate to God by merely observing daily, weekly, monthly, or annual ceremonies. Instead, a person would honor him by living a life that reflects godly principles. That is what Jesus spells out during this episode. Here he explains the kind of dedicated lifestyle that, from God's perspective, serves as worship (cf. Romans 12: 1).

Some have insisted that, while Matthew portrays this as a single teaching incident, this is really a case of the apostle offering a synopsis of teachings the disciples received from Jesus over the course of his ministry. Fueling this view is the fact that Mark and Luke present many of the teachings contained in the sermon much differently than Matthew. While Luke does record a setting that parallels Matthew's and includes many of the same teachings, some of the lessons taught on this occasion are scattered throughout the gospels of Mark and Luke. This could explain why, in Matthew's account, part of the message appears to be delivered only to his disciples while other aspects seem to involve a larger audience.

These things having been said, there is no question that the lessons captured in this sermon flow more smoothly in Matthew than they do in the other gospels. Additionally, according to Luke, Matthew was selected as a disciple just prior to Jesus' deliverance of this sermon. Thus, Matthew would have been one of those present at the time (Luke 6: 12-19), which means he was giving eye-witness testimony. Therefore, in this work the focus will be on Matthew's presentation of the *Sermon on the Mount*.

While some of these teachings are offered in various settings in Mark and Luke, it seems reasonable to believe that Jesus continued teaching these same godly principles throughout his ministry.

---

[1] Carson, D. A., *The Expositors Bible Commentary with the New International Version, Matthew Chapters 1 through 12*, Zondervan Publishing House, Grand Rapids, MI, 1995, pp 128-129.

Teaching something in this particular setting would not preclude Jesus from repeating those or similar words on other occasions to other listeners. Additionally, the apostle seems to leave the impression of a singular setting for the sermon with his follow-up remarks, stating, [28]"When Jesus had finished these words, the crowds were amazed at His teaching; [29]for He was teaching them as *one*[2] having authority, and not as their scribes" (Matthew 7: 28-29).

The content of the lessons shared in Jesus' sermon is eye-opening. Jesus boldly challenged the relational concepts by which humankind had lived for centuries (e.g., an eye for an eye), offering a fresh, godly look at both physical and spiritual relationships. He explained how God sees people and how God wants humanity to relate to him and to each other. With the covenant of grace on the horizon, it was important for him to set the bar a bit higher so that mankind might better understand what it means to live by faith.

---

[2] Italicized words are not found in the original Greek, but have been added to the English translation for easier reading.

Table of Contents

Title	Page

Chapter One

Matthew 5: 1-12

The Setting

Where the *Sermon on the Mount* is concerned, most people seem to imagine Jesus on perhaps a very high hill as throngs of people sat or stood on the downward slope listening to his words. However, the picture Matthew offers is a bit different, stating that, [1]"When Jesus saw the crowds, He went up on the mountain; and after He sat down, His disciples came to Him. [2]He opened His mouth and *began* to teach them…" (vv. 1-2).

While large crowds had followed Jesus, the sermon itself seems to have taken place in a much more private setting, or at least it began that way, with Jesus and his disciples separated from the multitudes who had followed him. Luke offers some additional insight, reporting the choosing of the twelve disciples who would later become apostles just a short time before this incident. Still, it is highly likely that more than the twelve were present even in the more removed setting since a number of other disciples shared intimately in Jesus' ministry here on earth (Acts 1: 21-22).

It is believed by a number of bible scholars that the setting for this sermon was a mount known as The Horns of Hattin, which is located about seven miles southwest of Capernaum. This site is well known for the Battle of Hattin, which was fought during the crusades. That battle, which took place in 1187 A.D., was arguably one of the most disastrous battles for the crusaders, effectively ending what was known at the time as the Kingdom of Jerusalem.

Others place the sermon closer to the city of Capernaum on Mount Eremos overlooking the Lake of Gennesaret. In fact, today it is called the Mount of Beatitudes, having been so named by those who insist that it is the true site of Jesus' sermon. Most will recognize *the beatitudes* as the popular name given to the first several verses of Jesus' discourse. In the 4th century A.D., a Byzantine church structure was built near Mount Eremos. Today there is a Roman Catholic building at this location known as the Church of the Beatitudes.

Another possible location is Arbel Mountain, which is a true mountain when compared to the lower hillsides of Hattin and Eremos. It lies further west and is substantially taller than the others. It is said that Napoleon's men believed this was the location of the Sermon on the Mount. The Sea of Galilee is almost completely visible from the summit of this mountain.

The specific locations of significant biblical events (e.g., Moses' burial place, the upper room, Jesus' tomb etc.) may be hidden deliberately. It could be that God wanted to discourage the enshrining and worship of such places since it could easily distract from the kind of worship he demands. Worship should never focus on earthly vessels or places.

It is noteworthy that Jesus sat down prior to teaching. In the modern age, it is not uncommon for a teacher or speaker to stand (perhaps on a platform or stage) while his listeners sit. However, throughout much of history, it is the teacher who would sit while those listening, and hopefully learning, would generally stand. This arrangement was intentional, depicting the teacher in a position of authority over his listeners. Therefore, it is likely that the disciples were standing before him.

Interestingly, the larger crowd seems to be part of the latter portions of this sermon (Matthew 7: 28). It seems reasonable to infer that the contents of chapter five, which constitute the beginning of the sermon, were geared toward a more intimate group, where Jesus referred to them as "…the salt of the earth" (v. 13) and "…the light of the world" (v. 14). In contrast, in chapters six and seven Jesus appears to be speaking to greater crowds to address a wider range of topics.

The Beatitudes

Jesus began his teaching with what are commonly referred to as *the beatitudes* (vv. 3-12), commenting on the blessed nature of certain individuals. In these verses he described for his followers what constitutes a blessed, or happy, life. The word *makarioi* literally means *happy,* or *fortunate,* but is translated as *blessed* in most English versions of the bible.

A large number of scholars like to apply the meaning of *happy* to the word *makarioi* in this setting, since it is a legitimate meaning of the word. However, the happiness they have in mind is not happiness as the term is generally used. That is to say, it is not happiness in the sense of cheerfulness or elation. After all, the poor in spirit (v. 3) or those who mourn (v. 4) could hardly be accused of living in a joyous state.

Perhaps the best meaning that could be assigned here is that expressed by the word *fortunate*. Some might question this meaning thinking that *fortunate* equates to *being lucky*, but that is not the meaning that is intended here. These individuals are fortunate in a very different sense. Adam Clarke, who employs the term *happy* in his commentary, makes note of the condition of those Jesus had in view, stating:

> …the person whom Christ terms happy is one who is not under the influence of *fate* or *chance*, but is governed by an all-wise *providence*, having every step directed to the attainment of *immortal glory*, being transformed by the *power* into the *likeness* of the ever-blessed God.[3]

From a limited human perspective, it is difficult to think of these people as fortunate, but that seems to be the message Jesus was trying to convey. Those who live in what many would consider less than blissful conditions are fortunate, spiritually speaking, despite what many would consider difficult circumstances. That is because spiritual fortune is not about one's circumstances; it is about character/attitude. In fact, those discussed here may not be fully aware of their good fortune since spiritual benefits are often difficult for people to appreciate while residing in this human state.

With his presentation of the beatitudes, Jesus seemed to serve up God's definition of righteousness. In other words, they offer some insight into the characteristics of a righteous person. While certain individuals in the Old Testament were deemed to be righteous (e.g. Genesis 6: 9; 15: 6), or recognized for their righteous actions, this passage offers insight into what constitutes a righteous person.

The Poor in Spirit

The beatitudes represent a departure from conventional human thought. Most people believe that being happy, or fortunate, means

---

[3] Clarke, Adam, *The Adam Clarke Commentary*,
http://classic.studylight.org/com/acc/view.cgi?book=mt&chapter=005,
accessed 01/15/2017

facing fewer challenges in life. Health and wealth are often considered a good measure of how fortunate one is. However, Jesus offered his disciples a contrary view of what constitutes the fortunate life. For instance, according to Jesus, it is "…the poor in spirit" who are fortunate (v. 3). What does it mean to be poor in spirit? The term, at its heart, points to humility. One who is poor in spirit recognizes his/her lowly position as a created being, who, but by God's grace, has no standing before him. It is the subservient – the lowly – that Jesus referred to here as *poor in spirit*. In the covenant of grace, these are people who are honest with themselves, recognizing their own spiritual bankruptcy and the futility of trying to escape it through their own personal effort.

Outwardly, mankind generally looks down at those who are humble (though they secretly tend to respect them for their humility). Instead, it is the proud, the wealthy, and those who seem to have the world by the tail that others envy for their positions of power and influence. Yet, according to Jesus, it is the opposing character – the humble person – who is the fortunate one. He is fortunate in that he has the kind of character God looks for when seeking those with whom he will share his kingdom.

The poor in spirit, who live in a state of humility, put little stock in earthly possessions. Losing everything they own would not be their undoing as it would be with most of humankind. While health and wealth may seem to be of great benefit here on earth and help someone gain superficial respect from men, God is not so easily impressed. He appreciates those who find satisfaction in things spiritual rather than temporal, and it is these with whom he wants to share eternal blessings.

Those Who Mourn

Next, Jesus told his disciples that "…those who mourn" are also fortunate (v. 4). This seems contrary to human nature since grief, or sorrow, is something most seek to avoid. Why, then, would Jesus consider one who mourns to be fortunate?

Jesus was not talking here about mourning over the loss (death) of a loved one or any of a host of assorted experiences common to men that tend to bring sorrow. Most scholars agree that the sorrow of which Jesus spoke is the godly sorrow about which the apostle Paul wrote (2 Corinthians 7: 11). It is the person who is able to see sin as God sees sin and, as a result, grieves over his own sinfulness and for the lost world around him.

Some may think it strange that Jesus would describe "...those who mourn" as fortunate. Yet, according to Jesus, they are fortunate in that "...they shall be comforted" (v. 4). While that sounds promising, most would prefer not to grieve in the first place rather than face the need for comfort. However, the comfort Jesus had in mind is not physical comfort, but spiritual and eternal comfort. One who carries such a burden for mankind's relationship with God is considered fortunate in that he/she will eventually see God and humankind reconciled in the heavenly kingdom. Temporal sorrow will be turned to delight as men share eternal joy with God in heaven.

The Gentle

Jesus continued, telling the disciples that "the gentle" are also fortunate (v. 5). Perhaps the English word that best expresses Jesus' use of gentle is the word *meek*. This is the translation found in certain other English versions (i.e., KJV, NIV, NKJV, NRSV, RSV, etc.). It is the submissive – the modest – the patient – about whom Jesus was speaking. It is people who are like Jesus – those who are generally free from malice or pretentiousness. They do not boast of their own accomplishments. They avoid self-glorification and generally dismiss accolades from other people. Instead, they tend to fill the role of a support person who seeks to help others do their best.

It is the gentle who "...will inherit the earth" (v. 5). The phrasing may seem a bit peculiar and those who have spent time parsing the words have differing views about the finer points of this terminology. However, a large number of bible scholars agree that the statement likely carries a dual meaning. For instance, Coffman states:

> *Inherit the earth*...does not refer exclusively to the 'new heaven and the new earth' (2 Peter 3: 13), but to this present earth as well. This is not a mere prophecy that the Christians shall be the landed gentry; but it is a statement that their relationship to the earth and its possessions shall be such as to bring them the greatest possible benefit and enjoyment of it.[4]

---

[4] Coffman, James B., *James Burton Coffman Commentaries – Matthew*, ACU Press, Abilene, TX, 1974, p 53.

The following comparable view is expressed in the *Zondervan Illustrated Bible Backgrounds Commentary, Volume 1*:

This perhaps recalls the lowly position before others found in the reference in Isaiah 61: 1, 3. Ultimately this points to the reign of Christ on earth (25: 35), but even now Jesus' disciples have entered into their spiritual inheritance.[5]

The most reasonable connection here seems to be with an Old Testament passage in the Psalms:

[9] For evildoers will be cut off,
But those who wait for the LORD, they will inherit the land.
[10] Yet a little while and the wicked man will be no more;
And you will look carefully for his place and he will not be *there*.
[11] But the humble will inherit the land
And will delight themselves in abundant prosperity. (Psalm 37: 9-11)

In this instance, David was writing about the reward for faithfulness. Coffman recognizes that the meek will experience "the greatest possible benefit" from life on earth. However, he does not explain *why* this is the case. The truth is that those who are meek tend to seek and need little to realize happiness/contentment with this life. For them, contentment is a way of life and not a goal to be accomplished. For instance, Paul told the Philippians:

[11]...for I have learned to be content in whatever circumstances I am.
[12] I know how to get along with humble means, and I also know how to live in prosperity; in any and every circumstance I have learned the secret of being filled and going hungry, both of having abundance and suffering need. (Philippians 4: 11-12)

Since the meek generally tend to seek little personal gratification from this life – at least, far less than many people – it stands to reason that they would fully appreciate everything they do have. If they are satisfied with modest housing, a humble automobile, and perhaps a less than elaborate cuisine for a diet, they consider themselves abundantly blessed when they have what others might consider unacceptable. The meek person rejoices over something that the

---

[5] Arnold, Clinton E., Editor, *Zondervan Illustrated Bible Backgrounds Commentary, Volume 1*, Zondervan Publishing, Grand Rapids, MI, 2002, p. 34.

arrogant person finds demeaning and contemptible. This is why, as Coffman states, the meek person attains "the greatest possible benefit and enjoyment" from God's blessings.

Those Who Hunger and Thirst after Righteousness

Among the most blessed, according to Jesus, "...are those who hunger and thirst for righteousness" (v. 6). This is a statement about people who *seek* godliness. Those who live in this age of grace are fortunate given the availability of the fullness of Scripture. It is true that those in the Old Testament had the prophets who delivered God's message and others spoke with him directly. Additionally, later generations had the Old Testament for guidance. However, in this day and age, men have been afforded much keener insight into how God thinks and what he expects from those who would walk with him. He has put aside every obstacle that has separated mankind from him over the centuries.

Other than Jesus (Isaiah 53: 11), only a handful of people in Scripture were ever called *righteous*. This includes men like Noah (Genesis 6: 9), Abraham (Genesis 15: 6), Moses, (Deuteronomy 9: 4); David (1 Kings 3: 6), Lot (2 Peter 2: 7) and Cornelius (Acts 10: 22). These are examples of people who hungered after righteousness. While others like Daniel and many of the Old Testament prophets undoubtedly lived what most would consider righteous lives, they were never given this designation in God's Word. This demonstrates God's sparing use of the term when it came to humankind. Righteousness is a term not easily applied to people because of sins committed.

What is interesting about Cornelius is that he was living a righteous life in the church age with little, if any, knowledge about Jesus. He was a Gentile and a Centurion in the Roman army. Consequently, his knowledge about the God of the Jews would have been limited. It seems that what really set Cornelius apart was his hunger for righteousness. He desired to live a life that honored God despite his seemingly restricted access to information about God.

Humans naturally have two strong cravings...one physical and one spiritual. Physical matters (food, relationships, etc.) sustain mankind physically and spiritual matters (Scripture, prayer, godly relationships with other people, etc.) sustain spiritually. Unfortunately, these two hungers play tug-of-war, each one wanting to be primary. As such, there is constant struggle between physical and spiritual wants and needs. It is this very idea that prompted Jesus to tell the crowd later in this same sermon that one cannot successfully serve two masters (Matthew 6: 24). Some people will ultimately give in to their physical needs/desires, making this physical life their master, while others will choose to focus on things spiritual, keeping physical needs in their proper, less significant place. Clarke put it plainly, writing:

> Heavenly things cannot support the *body*; they are not suited to its nature: *earthly* things cannot support the *soul*, for the same reason.[6]

When speaking about people "...who hunger and thirst for righteousness," Jesus stated that the reason they are blessed, or fortunate, is that their hunger and thirst would be satisfied. Fulfillment of this promise is seen in God's dealings with Cornelius. He was a man who sought after God. Indeed, he hungered and thirsted after righteousness...doing his best to live a righteous life with limited knowledge about what that meant. For this effort he was rewarded as God sent an apostle to satisfy his desire to learn (Acts 10: 22-48). All those who know that kind of earnest spiritual hunger can, according to Jesus, anticipate similar results.

The Merciful

It is interesting to see how closely the beatitudes parallel the thoughts expressed in the following verse from the Old Testament:

> He has shown you, O mortal, what is good. And what does the LORD require of you? To act justly and to love mercy and to walk humbly with your God. (Micah 6: 8, NIV)

In this verse, the prophet Micah has revealed God's expectations of humanity in much the same way Jesus laid out those expectations in the beatitudes. These two passages offer insight into the character of a godly person. To this point, the focus has been on aspects of that character that seem to correspond with the humility factor (i.e., the poor in spirit, those who mourn, those who are meek) and the matter of acting justly (hungering after righteousness). Next Jesus addressed the characteristic that is the showing of mercy (v. 7).

---

[6] Clarke, Adam, *The Adam Clarke Commentary*,
http://classic.studylight.org/com/acc/view.cgi?book=mt&chapter=005,
accessed 01/15/2017.

Mankind's reconciliation with God could not take place without mercy. He has taken the penalties for sin upon himself, making it possible for people to walk with him. If then, godliness is the goal, it cannot be realized without showing mercy to others. Jesus serves as a prime example of what it means to be merciful in that he gave his life to wash away sins. The converse is the example of the unmerciful servant who, in the end, was denied the mercy that he denied to others (Matthew 18: 21-35).

According to Jesus, the one who shows mercy will receive mercy in kind. It is safe to say that the godly person who shows mercy to others may well receive mercy worth much more than he/she has given. This would have been the case in Jesus' parable of the unmerciful servant, had he had any inclination to be merciful. For the believer who shows mercy as a matter of honoring God, the reciprocating mercy will be immeasurable. It will be received in the form of spiritual/eternal blessings rather than limited temporal mercy that lasts only for a while.

Mercy is not strictly about forgiveness. It also involves compassionate acts of kindness, such as serving those less fortunate than oneself. Giving to someone when nothing is owed, in contrast to forgiving what is owed, is considered a merciful act. For instance, almsgiving (providing for the poor) would have been considered a form of mercy. Showing mercy is a matter of treating with godly respect those to whom nothing is owed. When Jesus spoke of *the merciful*, he undoubtedly meant for the words to entail much more than simply forgiving a debt.

The Pure in Heart

Historically, God has placed a premium on the idea of cleanliness. For instance, for the Israelites, some animals were considered clean and, therefore, edible, while others were considered unclean. Through the Old Testament, assorted circumstances, such as touching a dead body, could place one in an unclean state where God was concerned (cf. Numbers 19: 11). The Old Testament is also riddled with ceremonies that were intended to provide outward cleansing (cf. Leviticus 14).

The problem with the various cleansing rituals of the Mosaic Law is that outward cleansing does nothing for one's inward uncleanness. It was always God's desire to commune with those who were inwardly clean rather than those who had simply practiced bathing rituals that provided superficial cleansing. God wants men to have pure (clean) hearts.

Purity of heart does not, as some might suspect, represent absolute sinless (clean) living. This cannot be what Jesus had in mind since every individual has sinned (Romans 3: 23). If *pure in heart* meant sinless living, it would be impossible for anyone to measure up. Instead, what Jesus seemed to have in mind is the principle of *circumcision of the heart* – a phrase used occasionally in God's Word. The idea of the circumcised heart is that it is a heart unimpeded in the person's walk with God. It is about unflagging openness and honesty/sincerity in one's relationship with God. When a person has developed this kind of honesty in his/her walk with God, it is God who, as a matter of faith on the part of the individual, provides the cleanness of heart necessary for a relationship with God to flourish. In response to a person's faith, he breaks down the barriers that have risen out of sin (Colossians 2: 11-13).

What will be the reward for the pure in heart? According to Jesus, "…they shall see God" (v. 8). Of course, no person can, in human form, witness God in his glory and live (Exodus 33: 20). There is, however, an eschatological promise that the faithful "…will see his face" (Revelation 22: 4). This must be at least part of what Jesus had in view with this statement. On the other hand, those who are pure in heart have the opportunity to see God to a certain degree even in this life. While men cannot see God in a physical sense, he has revealed his spiritual essence fully in his Word.

First of all, God can be clearly seen in the world he has created (Psalm 19: 1-4; Romans 1: 20). The pure in heart whose walk with God is unabated will appreciate this fact and see him in his creation. Second, he has revealed himself in the person of Jesus. Through faith, the pure in heart know Jesus, having shared in his death, and experienced the new life that is offered by his blood (Romans 6: 1-4). Also, he dwells in the hearts of the faithful (Romans 8: 11; 1 Corinthians 3: 16; 2 Corinthians 13: 5) and it is the pure in heart who are able to experience the fullness of his presence in their lives. Thus, they are able to commune with him on a very intimate level. Consequently, the pure in heart can see/experience God on a spiritual plane even as they remain flesh and blood here on earth.

The Peacemakers

Jehovah is a peaceful God. Paul recognized this, noting that he is "...the God of peace" (Philippians 4: 9) and the source of peace (Romans 5: 1) for the faithful. When the prophet Isaiah wrote concerning the coming Messiah, he called him '...the Prince of Peace' (Isaiah 9: 6). Similarly, God wants all of his children to be peaceful. He wants believers to be a source of peace, or peacemakers – bringing healing rather than divisiveness.

Peacemaking can be costly for the peacemaker in that it generally calls for a measure of humility. Later in the sermon, Jesus speaks of *turning the other cheek* when struck by another. This is certainly a strategy to gain peace, but it requires the setting aside of one's pride and submitting to an adversary. Therefore, the peacemaker commonly falls into the category of "...the poor in spirit" (v. 3) in that he/she is generally willing to set aside personal pride for the sake of peace.

Those individuals who, with all godly earnestness, seek to find peace for themselves and others "...shall be called sons of God" (v. 9). Take heart concerning this. It is no small matter to be called a son of God since these are the ones who are heirs to his kingdom in much the same way that a son is heir to his father's estate on earth, only on a much grander scale. Peacemakers, as sons of God, are the spiritual descendants of Abraham. This is the meaning of Paul's words to the Galatians when he stated:

> [26] For you are all sons of God through faith in Christ Jesus. [27] For all of you who were baptized into Christ have clothed yourselves with Christ. [28] There is neither Jew nor Greek, there is neither slave nor free man, there is neither male nor female; for you are all one in Christ Jesus. [29] And if you belong to Christ, then you are Abraham's descendants, heirs according to promise. (Galatians 3: 26-29)

Peacemakers, as heirs of the promise given to Abraham, can anticipate an eternal heavenly reward where they will be able to spend eternity in God's presence as his children.

The Persecuted

The persecuted are also considered fortunate since, like the poor in spirit (v. 3), "theirs is the kingdom of heaven" (v. 10). Those who are derided for their faith in God will be rewarded with an eternity in his spiritual haven. Having said this, Jesus applied this principle to the very disciples to whom he was speaking, telling them that they would be among the persecuted, stating:

> [11] Blessed are you when *people* insult you and persecute you, and falsely say all kinds of evil against you because of Me. [12] Rejoice and be glad, for your reward in heaven is great; for in the same way they persecuted the prophets who were before you. (Matthew 5: 11-12)

Notice that Jesus did not say *if* you are persecuted, but *when* you are persecuted. In other words, they could anticipate persecution. They could expect insults and false accusations. This is how the people treated the prophets of old.

The ways of the world naturally conflict with the ways of the godly. Consequently, they cannot co-exist harmoniously. While the godly may seek to live in harmony with the world, the worldly will reject peaceful efforts, seeking to force their own ways upon the godly. Still, there is no reason to despair. On the contrary, such persecution would be cause for rejoicing. It would give them the opportunity to stand for God in a meaningful way.

While the words of the Old Testament prophets were widely ignored by the people, the prophets themselves were persecuted for speaking on God's behalf. Some were even killed. Still, they stood boldly, unwilling to let anyone or anything stand between them and God. A similar pattern developed in the New Testament among the apostles, who were among those being addressed at this time. For instance, Peter and John were released from custody after having been threatened by the Jewish leaders in Jerusalem and warned that they must stop speaking about Jesus (Acts 4: 1-22). Upon their release, "…they went to their own *companions* and reported all that the chief priests and the elders had said to them. And when they heard *this*, they lifted their voices to God with one accord" (Acts 4: 23-24).

Similarly, Paul spent much of his ministry being persecuted for his faith and his teachings. He was imprisoned often, including his imprisonment in Philippi where he and Silas, from their cell block, sang praises to God (Acts 16: 25). The apostles evidently appreciated Jesus' words when he said that persecution for the sake of righteousness (v. 12) should be seen as a blessing and cause for rejoicing (v. 13).

Do not think of these *attitudes* as being apportioned to Christ's followers in the same way spiritual gifts are distributed to believers. It is not that some will be poor in spirit and others will be merciful. The characteristics described here speak to the character of a faithful believer. That is to say, the person who honors God with his/her life will be all of the above, at least to some degree. Jesus anticipates that his followers will be meek, merciful peacemakers who hunger after righteousness. Thus, these attitudes are not meant to be divided among believers, but present in each one.

Chapter Two

Matthew 5: 13-20

Salt of the Earth

Salt has various uses. In modern times, it is generally considered a seasoning that adds flavor to the foods people eat. However, historically there are four primary categories where the use of salt is concerned. As noted, it is used as a seasoning to enhance the flavor of food. Also, salt is used as a preservative for meat and other items. Additionally, it is employed as a drying agent to prepare (cure) certain items (tobacco, leather, etc.) for use. Finally, salt is used to soften water and melt ice.

The term "…covenant of salt" or "…salt of the covenant" appears three times in the Old Testament (Leviticus 2: 13; Numbers 18: 19; 2 Chronicles 13: 5). In the first two instances God commanded that any Israelite offering given to God was to be seasoned with salt, which was intended to represent the substantive, unending character of their covenant. On the third occasion God established his covenant of salt with David when he handed the kingdom of Israel over to the seed of David.

Salt is mentioned so much in Scripture, in both literal and figurative terms, that the time involved in a study on that topic would be prohibitive at this time. Still, here are a few examples of its use that offer a sense of the worth God saw in this substance.

He went out to the spring of water and threw salt in it and said, 'Thus says the Lord, "I have purified these waters; there shall not be from there death or unfruitfulness any longer."' (2 Kings 2: 21)

"[33] He changes rivers into a wilderness
And springs of water into a thirsty ground;
[34] A fruitful land into a salt waste,
Because of the wickedness of those who dwell in it.

³⁵ He changes a wilderness into a pool of water
And a dry land into springs of water;" (Psalm 107: 33-35)

Let your speech always be with grace, *as though* seasoned with salt, so that you will know how you should respond to each person. (Colossians 4: 6).

In modern times, refined salt sits in a container in nearly every cupboard of civilized nations. However, in times past salt was considered more precious. This explains why God included salt as part of the offerings he expected to receive from the Israelites (Ezra 6: 9). Salt was so highly valued that the people of many nations even paid their taxes with salt (Egypt, Greece, Rome, etc.). The numerous uses of salt give a sense of the worth of this substance during the first century when Jesus lived on earth.

Following his list of what are commonly known as the beatitudes (vv. 2-12), Jesus told his disciples, "You are the salt of the earth" (v. 13). With this statement, Jesus was explaining to his disciples that they were in the position of being fundamental to life itself in much the same way that salt is fundamental. Like salt, they had the capacity to enhance and preserve life for those on earth through the message they would carry to the world. According to B. W. Johnson, "Salt preserves from corruption"[7] and this is arguably Jesus' primary point. However, in order to be effective in that role, they must maintain their saltiness. They must resist becoming bland (worldly) and, as a result, incapable of fulfilling that fundamental role.

Light of the World

Jesus continued his thoughts, telling the disciples, "You are the light of the world" (v. 14). Light, which is a necessary ingredient for life on earth, equally illuminates one's immediate path and the entire world. It offers perspective concerning a person's position or destination and serves as a tool to guide people where they wish to go much like the star led the magi to Jesus.

Jesus used this *light of the world* terminology regarding himself, also. John wrote, "Then Jesus again spoke to them, saying, 'I am the Light of the world; he who follows Me will not walk in the darkness, but will have the Light of life.'" (John 8: 12). This begs the question: *If*

---

[7] Johnson, B. W., *The People's New Testament*, Gospel Light Publishing Co., Delight, AR, p. 36.

Jesus is the light of the world, in what sense are his followers the light of the world? A helpful analogy can be found in the relationship between the sun and the moon. The sun lights the daytime not just because it is brighter than the moon, but because it is the *source* of light. The moon, on the other hand, reflects the sun's light to help illuminate the darkness of night.

The apostle John writes much about the fact that the true disciples of Christ walk/live in the light, of which God is the source (1 John 1: 5). The goal of believers should be to reflect that light to unbelievers. Since Christians are the only Jesus unbelievers encounter on earth, the hope is that the light of Jesus that Christians reflect will illuminate their path in a dark world.

Jesus stated, "I am the way, and the truth, and the life; no one comes to the Father but through Me" (John 14: 6). Just as the light of a torch helps men to find their way out of darkness, it is upon believers to reflect the light of Jesus, enticing others to follow them to Jesus.

Light naturally attracts attention. When a candle is lit in a dark room, all eyes are automatically drawn to that light. The reason for this is that the candle contrasts the darkness by which it is surrounded. It also serves to shed light upon the surroundings that were so well-hidden inside that darkness.

In that same vein, when believers provide a different example to the world, one that contrasts their surroundings, like a candle in a dark room, they draw the attention of those lost in the darkness of the world. Additionally, they serve to shed light on the surroundings (evil) that were so well-hidden inside that world of darkness. This provides them with an opportunity to lead others to where Christ is – that is, to find *the way*.

Those who reflect the light of Jesus to others cannot help but be noticed. They will be too obvious to be ignored. Like a city that sits atop a hill (v. 14), everyone in the vicinity will recognize the marked disparity between the light of Christ and the darkness of the world.

The light of Jesus that shines through believers must be given every opportunity to provide clarity to all who are near. It must not be hidden. One does not light a candle to brighten a room and place the candle under a basket where it would not serve its purpose. Rather, it is placed on a lamp stand, or in some other prominent position, where it serves to provide light so that all can see (v. 15). In that same way, believers should not smother the flame of Jesus, which is reflected in their good works. When good works are done in Jesus' name, they are seen by the world and help the faithful to gain influence upon those watching. This influence can help believers to lead unbelievers to Jesus (v. 16).

A single candle can provide a small measure of light. However, a collection of candles, such as those placed together on a lamp stand, can light an entire room. A strong argument can be made that the lamp stand mentioned by Jesus (v. 15) represents the church in much the same way lamp stands are used to depict individual congregations in the apostle John's apocalyptic vision (Revelation 1:20). Just as the candles on a lamp stand supplement each other to collectively light a room, when believers join together in the work of the church, the light from each believer is joined with the light from other believers providing an intensity that can illuminate an entire community.

The Abrahamic Covenant

It is important to remember that it was the Jewish people whom Matthew sought to influence with his gospel. It is also important to note that this appears to be an early teaching opportunity for Jesus (within the first several months of his ministry). Therefore, his words are foundational in that he is attempting to introduce the disciples to principles of godliness. However, he is also trying to provide them with a big picture view of God's relationship with men, particularly where the Gentiles are concerned, since this was a lesson the Jews would need to learn.

With that in mind, Jesus quickly shifted gears. The next words out of his mouth were, "Do not think that I came to abolish the Law or the Prophets…" (v. 17). The phrase "the Law or the Prophets" is generally understood as a reference to the Mosaic Law and the Old Testament Scriptures after which the Jews sought to model their relationship with God. Since Jesus was introducing a new manner of walking with God, one that seemed to contrast the Law, he wanted to clarify that he was not here to abandon Old Testament teachings, but to fulfill them.

The Old Testament is essentially 39 books that were intended to lay the groundwork for Christ's coming and the ensuing covenant of grace. They were the *tutor* mentioned by the apostle Paul (Galatians 3: 25) meant to prepare mankind for the covenant of grace. With Jesus' arrival, God began to fulfill the prophecies/promises of the Old Testament. That is why Jesus stated, "I did not come to abolish but to fulfill" (v. 17). The Old Testament was, in essence, God's covenant with the Jews. The promise of that covenant was God's assurance to Abraham that, "…in you all the families of the earth will be blessed" (Genesis 12: 3). Jesus' arrival marked the beginning of the fulfillment of that promise. Thus, Jesus was not abandoning the law, as some suspected. Instead, he came to satisfy the terms/promises of that covenant.

While the Old and New Testaments are generally discussed in terms of old and new covenants, it is fair to say that this is not quite what God had in mind. The New Testament does not offer a new covenant, *per se*, but offers a covenant that is intended to fulfill the promises of the first covenant. Thus, Jesus' arrival was not the end of the first covenant, where the children of Israel were God's chosen; but it does provide superior definition of what constitutes the seed of Abraham, Isaac, and Jacob in God's eyes. The New Testament accomplishes God's long-term plans for the Abrahamic covenant. This is why the Abrahamic covenant is called "an everlasting covenant" (Genesis 17: 7). It is a covenant that will not be fully discharged until the (spiritual) seed of Abraham are united with Christ at the Second Coming. According to Paul:

> "[6] But it is not as though the word of God has failed. For they are not all Israel who are *descended* from Israel; [7] nor are they all children because they are Abraham's descendants, but: "THROUGH ISAAC YOUR DESCENDANTS WILL BE NAMED." [8] That is, it is not the children of the flesh who are children of God, but the children of the promise are regarded as descendants." (Romans 9: 6-8)

The Old Testament is relevant even in modern times – not that modern men are held to the specific terms of that covenant, but they are living its fulfillment. For instance, blood sacrifice is still required to cover sins, but the nature of the blood sacrifice has changed (Hebrews 9: 12). Similarly, the tabernacle – God's dwelling place among men – has seen a transformation. God no longer dwells in a man-made tabernacle, but in a "…tabernacle, not made with hands" (Hebrews 9: 11), which is the hearts of men (cf. 2 Corinthians 1: 22).

The Old Testament provides much insight into how God thinks and works. Godly principles, demonstrated throughout the Old Testament, provide instruction concerning man's relationship with him. The Mosaic Law, and particularly the Ten Commandments, offer guidance that transcends time. Therefore, the lessons of the Old Testament are too valuable to simply be discarded.

How does this harmonize with Paul's teaching that mankind no longer lives under the dictates of the Mosaic Law? This is answered a number of times in the New Testament, including a few passages that have already been mentioned here (Galatians 3: 25; Romans 9: 6-8; Hebrews 9: 11-12). The ninth and tenth chapters of Hebrews offer an expanded understanding of what Paul had in mind. While the New Testament places modern men in the position of living the fulfillment of the old covenant, it is also a covenant within itself. Certain elements of the Abrahamic covenant were replaced with new covenant ideas. For instance, people now worship Jehovah "...in spirit and truth" (John 4: 23) as opposed to the assorted worship rituals defined in the law. Also, salvation is by grace based on the blood sacrifice of Jesus. Consequently, the continuing animal sacrifices of the Old Testament have been discarded.

It is important to remember that the Mosaic Law was intended as a *tutor* (cf. Galatians 3: 23-25) that would provide direction and insight. It was meant to be foundational and was specific to the relationship between God and the Jews. The Mosaic Law was never intended to apply to Gentiles in that same sense. It is this foundational nature of that covenant that makes it so relevant today. If a building lacks a solid foundation, the structure crumbles. While modern men are not held to the minute details of the law, they are expected to recognize the fundamental godly instruction (the foundation) it has to offer and live accordingly.

The church age is a time of fulfillment of the Abrahamic covenant. That Jesus did not completely discharge the terms of that covenant is found in his words, "...until heaven and earth pass away, not the smallest letter or stroke shall pass from the Law until all is accomplished" (v. 18). This means that the spirit of the Abrahamic covenant will remain in effect until it realizes eschatological (end times) fulfillment at the Second Coming of Christ.

The godly principles of the Old Testament are to be embraced by the seed of Abraham. New Testament believers are not only to abide by, but to teach these principles. In fact, one could legitimately argue that, in New Testament times, the seed of Abraham are held to a higher standard where godly principles are concerned, since those in the church age have been offered considerably greater insight into the things of God than were the Israelites of old. This is reflected in the teachings found not only through the New Testament, but specifically here in the *Sermon on the Mount*, where he raises the bar for those who seek to walk with God.

Misapplying the Law

The scribes and Pharisees sought to model their worship of God after Old Testament teachings. However, they evidently considered those teachings inadequate in providing direction to the Israelites. Therefore, they developed a number of oral traditions by which they believed the Israelites should live. Later codified into what is known as the *Mishnah*, they hoped to teach the Israelites not only *to* obey the law, but *how* to obey the law. Thus, the commandment to honor the Sabbath came to mean that no one could perform any manual labor on the Sabbath.

The problem for the scribes and Pharisees is that they failed to grasp the spiritual intent of the law. For instance, keeping the Sabbath Day holy was not about limiting the distance one happened to travel on that particular day (the *Mishnah* limits this to a Sabbath Day's journey, or about 3/5 of a mile), but about honoring God with the things in which one participated. While the Sabbath was identified as a day of rest, it was not God's intent that *rest* should be quantified by distance traveled, making this one of the manmade rules for which Jesus often chided them (cf. Luke 11: 37-44). Thus, Jesus warned his followers, "...unless your righteousness surpasses *that* of the scribes and Pharisees, you will not enter the kingdom of heaven" (v. 20).

Chapter Three

Matthew 5: 21-48

Redefining Obedience

The realization that Jesus raised the bar for those who, in the covenant of grace, seek to have a relationship with God is seen in the balance of the *Sermon on the Mount*. Over the ensuing verses, a number of times Jesus employed the terms, "You have heard...but I say." In each instance where these words are used, Jesus juxtaposed elements of the Mosaic Law and common human experience against life in the covenant of grace. Mankind's relationship with God is redefined in the new covenant with expectations far surpassing the provisions of the law as Jesus taught and hoped that the righteousness of his followers would surpass that of the scribes and Pharisees (v. 20).

Anger

Addressing what many consider the most grievous of sins, Jesus began his redefinition of godliness by touching on the topic of murder – the unjustified taking of another human life. In this case, the "You have heard..." portion of his statement is that "You shall not commit murder" (v. 21). However, Jesus raised the bar for his listeners, explaining to them that, while murder is not insignificant, it is the insufferable attitude that leads to murder that must be addressed since, absent that attitude, no murder would be committed. It is anger toward one another for which people will be held accountable, even when it does not result in physical murder or other heinous crimes.

It would be a mistake to read the crimes and accountability mentioned by Jesus as *degrees* of crimes and accountability. Notwithstanding human crime and punishment, Jesus stated that "...everyone who is angry with his brother shall be guilty before the court" (v. 22). He followed with, "whoever says to his brother, 'You good-for-nothing,' shall be guilty before the supreme court" (v. 22).

Again, he explained that "…whoever says, 'You fool,' shall be guilty *enough to go* into the fiery hell" (v. 22). Some may see these statements as diminishing or escalating degrees of crime/sin, but that does not seem to be the case. Instead, Jesus was reiterating, in threefold fashion, the distinction between a temporal crime (v. 21) and a spiritual sin (v. 22). Words spewed in anger are unacceptable where God is concerned, regardless of the circumstances.

A human court may find a person guilty of murder and prescribe a punishment for the crime. However, God judges the heart. That is to say, he holds each individual accountable for the anger/hate in his/her heart. For one guilty of such hate, the consequences are much more substantive than any punishment a human court might render. Unlike the temporal punishment meted out by a judge, the consequences for the kind of hate Jesus described here are spiritual and eternal. While a man's life may be taken from him as a result of his crime, the punishment beyond this life for the unrepentant soul is spiritual death – permanent separation from God and eternal punishment in "the fiery hell" (v. 22).

The hatefulness addressed here by Jesus is foreign to the person who loves God. He not only does not hate his brother, but he loves others as God loves them. Still, that does not mean that men never experience challenges in their relationships. Indeed, they do. Therefore, Jesus offered some wise words for his listeners. For the one who may have had a falling out with another, that person should seek reconciliation since the breach in that relationship dishonors God. If one wishes to present an offering to God or to worship God in some fashion, a falling out with a brother or sister is a problem for God (v. 23). Consequently, that person should straightaway seek reconciliation with all humility. Once reconciled in godly fashion, the offering can be presented to God honorably, untainted by unseemly distractions (v. 24). It is impossible for someone to honor God on Sunday in conjoined worship with others if that same person's activities throughout the week dishonor him (cf. Romans 12: 1-2).

Reconciling with Others

Jesus continued his teaching, offering some common-sense thoughts about relationships. For instance, it is unwise, according to Jesus, to allow relationships to sour and fail. The life of a believer should be lived in a manner that offends no one. If, however, someone wants to sue a believer for what they see as an offense, the wisest decision is to settle out of court. It is likely that an out-of-court settlement will be much more acceptable than a decision handed down by a judge (vv. 25-26) and this does not even take into consideration the court/legal expenses one might incur. If a believer has, indeed, wronged someone even inadvertently, not only may he/she pay a much higher price as a result of a lawsuit, but refusal to settle will likely destroy the possibility of reconciliation with the person who believes they have been harmed. The relationships of God's faithful, even relationships with unbelievers, should be grounded in godliness rather than legalities.

Although Jesus did not specifically state it here, it stands to reason that the reverse situation also holds true. In other words, a believer who has been harmed by another should not seek settlement in court. If restitution is due, it should be sought outside of the courts so that the relationship might be preserved. In fact, rather than seeking settlement, forgiveness should be the believer's response. For the Christian, relationship is much more important than worldly goods and any satisfaction one might receive through redress.

Some may think it unusual that Jesus would so boldly address the human legal system in his lesson, but his teaching is not about the courts. His teaching is about the human heart and the fact that, where Christians are concerned, relationships must always come first. In the courts, those relationships tend to break down rapidly and, consequently, do not serve God's purpose well.

Adultery

Jesus repeated his "You have heard…but I say" mantra in connection with adultery. The seventh commandment states, "You shall not commit adultery" (Exodus 20: 14). However, Jesus again raised the bar for those who wish to have a relationship with God in the covenant of grace. Rather than condemning the act of adultery, Jesus condemned what might be termed *adultery of the heart*. That is to say, even the *desire* to commit adultery dishonors God. According to Jesus, the man who merely lusts after a woman "has already committed adultery with her in his heart" (v. 28).

If Your Right Eye Makes You Stumble

The next verses give a sense of the irrelevance of one's physical life weighed against the significance of spiritual life. For instance, Jesus stated, "If your right eye makes you stumble, tear it out and throw it from you" (v. 29). What would lead him to make such a biting remark? The words are spoken in connection with a person's spiritual health. The idea is that one should not allow anything to stand in the way where a relationship with God is concerned. It is on the shoulders of each individual to do what is necessary to preserve that relationship since one's eternal fortune depends on it. Jesus offered these words on the heels of his comment on *adultery of the heart*, so it is not unreasonable to seek a connection there. The man who sees a woman and lusts after her would be better off to lose his sight and remove the temptation. Why? Losing one's sight is a mere inconvenience when compared to losing one's eternal salvation.

The same idea is offered with respect to one's right hand (v. 30). If a person's right hand leads to actions that dishonor God, cut it off and throw it away. Here the logic is the same. Losing one's right hand, or any other bodily part, is a mere physical inconvenience when compared to losing one's eternal salvation. The reason is that spiritual salvation is infinitely more significant than the temporal conveniences of this life.

Divorce

Some may consider Jesus' next words intrusive, mostly because they are. It may be relatively easy for someone to shrug off the notion of cutting out an eye or cutting off a hand, deeming these to be inflated statements that are intended to emphasize the insignificance of life on earth when compared to eternal salvation. However, Jesus now turns to the topic of divorce, which hits quite close to home for many. Under the law, divorce was allowed as a matter of severing the marital bond. However, even though divorce was *accepted* under the law (v. 31), it was never *acceptable* where God was concerned. Jesus identifies divorce, with the exception of a circumstance of unfaithfulness, as dishonoring God. That is the way God has always viewed divorce. It is the breaking of a covenant that God has sanctioned.

Within the framework of his discussion about divorce, Jesus tossed in the word *adultery*. According to Jesus, a man who divorces his wife "makes her commit adultery" (v. 32), unless, of course, her own commitment of adultery is what led to divorce. This may raise concerns that the innocent woman in a divorce might be viewed as an adulteress through no fault of her own. The phrase certainly seems to render a peculiar verdict against an innocent.

This verse can be viewed through various lenses. The English translation "...commit adultery" appears to use the term in an active sense. However, the Greek *moichasthai* from which the translation derives is passive and might be better translated *makes her an adulteress*. *The Pulpit Commentary* states that the term "connotes being sinned against rather than sinning."[8]

Gill offers a different explanation, stating, "...causeth her to commit adultery; that is, as much as in him lies: should she commit it, he is the cause of it, by exposing her, through a rejection of her, to the sinful embraces of others."[9] In other words, Jesus was not saying that she would be guilty of adultery but that, having been forced to participate in divorce, any intimate relationship she might have with a man afterward would necessarily be outside the covenant of her original marriage. By this he means that the man has caused her to experience and participate in the breaking of a covenant. If the man has already broken the covenant due to his own unfaithfulness that may excuse the woman from the marriage, but the wife is still party to a broken covenant even as the innocent party.

The verse is about a woman being unjustifiably divorced. With that in mind, Brian Bell wrote, "Jesus seems to indicate that **sexual infidelity** is an acceptable reason for divorce; all other reasons render subsequent marriages *adulterous* (biblical divorce vs. non-biblical divorce)."[10] Coke's view appears to be similar to that of Bell. He wrote, "...he who divorces his wife for any of the causes allowed by the doctors, *whoredom* excepted, layeth her under a strong temptation to commit adultery; unjust divorce being no divorce in the sight of God: and that since such marriages still subsisted, he who married the woman unjustly divorced, committeth adultery also."[11]

In similar fashion, marrying someone who has been divorced – save in the case where the divorce was due to marital infidelity – is

[8] Exell, Joseph S., Spence-Jones, Henry, editors, *Pulpit Commentary*, http://biblehub.com/commentaries/pulpit/matthew/5.htm, accessed March 3, 2017.
[9] Gill, John, *John Gill's Exposition of the Whole Bible*, https://www.studylight.org/commentaries/geb/matthew-5.html, accessed March 6, 2017.
[10] Bell, Brian, *Brian Bell Commentary on the Bible*, https://www.studylight.org/commentaries/cbb/matthew-5.html, accessed March 20, 2017.
[11] Coke, Thomas, *Thomas Coke Commentary on the Holy Bible*, https://www.studylight.org/commentaries/tcc/matthew-5.html, accessed March 20, 2017.

seen through the eyes of God as another manner in which the marriage covenant is broken. Presuming a marriage is ended due to unfaithfulness, Jesus' remark concerning remarriage does not seem to be pointed at the innocent party. Concerning this, McGarvey wrote:

> It is clearly implied...that the marriage bond is broken; and it is almost universally conceded by commentators and moralists that the innocent party to such a divorce can marry again.[12]

One of the reasons most scholars agree with McGarvey's assessment is that this view is supported later in Matthew's gospel. The Pharisees were constantly attempting to trap Jesus into saying something that would alienate some of his followers. At the time there was a divide among the Israelites concerning what constituted an acceptable reason for divorce. A segment of the populace sided with Hillel the Elder (110 BCD-10 CE) who had taught that a man could divorce his wife for any trivial reason (e.g., burning a meal). On the other hand, the Jewish scholar Shammai (50 BCE-30 CE), who was deeply involved in the development of the Jewish *Mishnah*, taught that divorce should be granted only for an especially egregious offense such as spousal unfaithfulness. In Jesus' exchange with the Pharisees on that occasion, he made the following comment.

> I tell you that anyone who divorces his wife, except for sexual immorality, and marries another woman commits adultery. (Matthew 19: 9)

Since the covenant of marriage would have already been broken by infidelity, Jesus recognized the freedom of the innocent party to divorce and remarry without committing adultery. This is what McGarvey and others have determined concerning Jesus' words in the *Sermon on the Mount*.

Over the course of time mankind had disrespected the covenant of marriage by making it easy and acceptable to obtain a divorce. Indeed, a man could divorce his wife if she burned his supper, though it is unlikely that this would be the actual reason for the divorce. It was this blatant disregard for the covenant that disturbed Jesus. In this segment

---

[12] McGarvey, J. W., *A Commentary on Matthew and Mark*, Gospel Light Publishing, Delight, AR, p. 56.

his intent was to teach that marriage should be returned to its elevated, God-ordained status.

Some may wonder why Jesus seemed to discuss marriage strictly in terms of the man's responsibility. In the first century, and even through most of history, men have been held accountable for most decision-making and familial activities. It is true that women can be, and are, held accountable, but until recently marriage was not generally addressed in terms of female responsibility. In fact, it is reasonable to believe that men, who were created first, are still held more accountable to God for these things. Paul teaches Timothy about this distinction in his first epistle to the young man (1 Timothy 2: 13), and there is no reason to believe this has changed, notwithstanding the modern-day secular perspective on the roles of men and women.

This begs the question: *How long will God hold someone accountable for the adultery of divorce or for the adultery of marrying a divorced person?* Does the guilt never subside? Is this the unforgivable sin? Once adultery has been committed or divorce has been given, since the person is living in what could be argued is a perpetual state of adultery, is it possible to reconcile with God?

It is safe to say that divorce is not the unforgivable sin Jesus discussed with his disciples. He told them "any sin and blasphemy shall be forgiven people, but blasphemy against the Spirit shall not be forgiven" (Matthew 12: 31). Divorce does not seem to rise to the same level as blasphemy of the Holy Spirit as Jesus described it. Still, as with any sin, repentance (recognition of the wrong accompanied by godly sorrow) should be offered to God for the decisions one has made. On the other hand, God would not want someone to obtain another divorce to correct the situation, which would seem to simply heap transgression upon transgression. As with other decisions that dishonor God, it is important to address it with him and seek forgiveness, recognizing it as a sin against him.

Married to an Unbeliever

In light of Jesus' words about divorce, what can be said about a marriage between a Christian and an unbeliever? Paul addresses this topic a couple of times in his epistles. Some rely on the words he wrote to the Corinthians to justify divorce (1 Corinthians 7: 13-15), but that is not Paul's intent. Taken in context, the overt theme of Paul's epistles is that men and women should remain faithful and married to their spouse, even when the spouse is an unbeliever. Peter's preference is that the spouse should be won over to Christ (1 Peter 3: 1). However, even if that does not happen, one's faithfulness to his/her spouse continues to honor God (1 Corinthians 7: 12-16), which was Jesus' point here in the *Sermon on the Mount*.

Taking an Oath

In discussing the making of *oaths*, Jesus appears to make reference to an Old Testament passage where the topic is addressed. However, the idea encompasses more than simply taking a vow or making a pledge. Consider these words from Leviticus.

> [11] You shall not steal, nor deal falsely, nor lie to one another. [12] You shall not swear falsely by My name, so as to profane the name of your God; I am the Lord. (Leviticus 19: 11-12)

While the Old Testament allowed for the taking of oaths, the warning is about breaking an oath, particularly if the oath is made in God's name. That having been said, the passage actually addresses the greater ideal of truthfulness/honesty, which is Jesus' focus in his words in the *Sermon on the Mount*. However, Jesus again raised the bar, telling his disciples that they should not only deal honestly with their fellowman, but they should avoid taking oaths of any kind (v. 34). In truth, an honest person has no need for an oath.

The Jews had a history of swearing an oath based on what they saw as their unique standing with God as his chosen people. Consequently, they may swear by heaven (God's throne) or by earth (God's footstool), evidently believing that it somehow enhanced their oath or pledge. What they failed to grasp is that no man, not even one of God's chosen, has the standing to swear by heaven or by earth or by anything created by God since, like Job, people had nothing to do with creation (Job 38). While humans were created in God's image in contrast to the balance of creation, mankind is still a part of that creation. Consequently, no individual has standing to use it in offering an oath.

What Jesus was discussing when it came to the idea of taking an oath was the effort by some to seek to overcome their own human frailty with a pledge or oath. The primary reason people are willing to offer an oath, or make a vow, is to give their words a sense of force. Yet, according to Jesus, if one's word is true, it does not need to be bolstered by an oath, nor would people demand it from an honest person. In that vein, Jesus stated "…let your statement be, 'Yes, yes' or 'No, no'; anything beyond these is of evil" (v. 37).

This would not preclude one from taking an oath of truthfulness before the court or offering wedding vows, since those are not the kind of oaths/vows Jesus had in mind. What Jesus had in view was honesty in daily living – honesty that manifests itself in such a way that one's trustworthiness would go unchallenged by those who know the person best. Still, there may be times when a Christian is in a position where a pledge might be necessary when dealing with the world. When that is the case, the believer honors any oath or pledge that is made, such as repayment of debt or any other circumstances where an agreement is made with someone who is outside of Christ.

Turn the Other Cheek

Jesus also proposed a change in a person's response to those who would do him harm. Rather than "…AN EYE FOR AN EYE, AND A TOOTH FOR A TOOTH" (v. 38), Jesus encouraged his followers to "…not resist an evil person" (v. 39). He went on to explain that his followers were to respond to others with Christ-like humility. For instance, should someone strike a believer on the cheek with his hand, no defense should be given and certainly no retaliation should be attempted. Instead, it should be considered an opportunity to display Christ-like humility by offering the other cheek.

This is a hard lesson to accept, especially since it is contrary to human nature. When attacked, a person's natural response is to offer some kind of defense. There is a tendency among men to react with equal, if not superior force when provoked or assailed. Note also that Jesus is not talking strictly about being struck by a brother/sister in the faith. His words speak to a Christian's response to an attack from anyone, not just believers where mutual faith in Christ might help overcome a normal reaction.

Give Your Coat Also

Jesus spoke about those who attack others, not spiritually or physically, but perhaps economically, legally, etc. For instance, when someone sues a believer, it is the character of the godly person to offer more than he/she is seeking. Hence, Jesus' statement, "If anyone wants to sue you and take your shirt, let him have your coat also" (v. 40). The order of the items mentioned here is significant.

According to the Mosaic Law, one's cloak was an incontrovertible possession (Exodus 22: 26-27; Deuteronomy 24: 13). In other words, a person's outer cloak need not be surrendered – ever. Even a court had no standing to relieve someone of his cloak to satisfy a debt. Yet Jesus suggested here that, while a cloak could not be *taken*, the believer should show a willingness to go well beyond what is required to settle a dispute, gladly offering up what the law said they could keep.

The logic behind this is twofold. First of all, it is unbecoming a Christian to become involved in legal wrangling. Second, it is well-known that legal proceedings are, in themselves, quite expensive, especially when the opportunity to avoid them is available. Still, this begs the question: *Should a believer surrender to someone who is suing him illegitimately?* Would that not simply encourage the culprit to engage in other unwarranted litigation? Also, what should be the believer's response if someone is seeking to completely destroy him financially without warrant? Perhaps part of the answer lies in the following observation by Coffman:

> This is exactly the same principle in another setting and is repeated for the sake of emphasis. Nor should too much be made of the fact that most of the losses in these verses seem rather trivial, a flick on the cheek, the loss of a coat, and going a mile. They do suggest, however, that there may be larger areas where the child of God may not use the 'submissive response' enjoined in these passages. God does not say, 'If one shall strike thy child, present the child's other cheek!'[13]

Coffman's point is interesting, noting "…that most of the losses in these verses seem rather trivial." He also observes that circumstances may arise when the *submissive response* is not the best choice – hence, his comment regarding a child's cheek. Jesus seemed to be speaking in terms of everyday living and not about unjustified lawsuits with the potential to wipe out one's entire estate. Of course, believers should be living lives where others are not inclined to sue them for anything, but the idea here seems to be more in the vein of relatively minor issues that happen in the course of ordinary life affording the godly person the opportunity to let Christ shine through. Jesus' point that believers should exemplify Christ in even the most difficult circumstances is

---

[13] Coffman, James B., *James Burton Coffman Commentaries-Matthew*, A.C.U. Press, Abilene, TX, 1974, p. 70

something that should be taken very seriously by those who love him and seek to lead others to him.

Going the Extra Mile

Jesus offered a third example of how one might relate to others with all godliness. He told the disciples "Whoever forces you to go one mile, go with him two" (v. 41). It was an accepted practice in the Roman Empire for Roman soldiers to commandeer civilians to assist them. They would commonly appeal to civilians to help them carry their load for a short time. The customary distance was a Roman mile (about 5,000 feet), which is just short of an English mile. However, Jesus again raised the bar suggesting that it would be most charitable to offer to carry the load beyond what was customary, thus allowing Christian charity to be seen by others.

Generosity

Similarly, he stated, "Give to him who asks of you, and do not turn away from him who wants to borrow from you" (v. 42). This is a bold statement, and one that could be very costly. He does not appear to qualify his remarks. For instance, he did not limit giving to those who are family members or those who are truly in need. Nor did he confine loaning to a particular group (e.g., brother or sisters in Christ). Instead, these seem to be rather broad statements about generosity and how one views his/her own possessions.

A person cannot give what he/she does not have. An example of this is found in Peter and John's encounter with a man who was disabled. The man sat outside the temple asking for donations (Acts 3: 3). Peter responded by telling the man they had no money to give, but he did have something to offer. With that, he healed the man (Acts 3: 6-7). Having no money did not prevent Peter from helping this man in other ways, which is another lesson that may be gleaned from Jesus' words. Still, to what extent are believers to be benevolent toward others? Should benevolence exceed what is affordable?

The lesson of Scripture is that Christians are to give as Christ gave. A number of examples are given. For instance, shortly after the church was established on the Day of Pentecost, many believers sold some of their assets and offered the proceeds to the apostles to be used to help those less fortunate (Acts 2: 44-45; 4: 36-37). Additionally, Jesus taught a lesson about giving as he and the disciples watched a widow place her last coin into the temple offering (Luke 21: 1-4).

What Jesus seemed to be teaching the disciples here in the *Sermon on the Mount* was that sacrificial giving should be seen as a fundamental aspect of the Christian life. Giving is steeped in faith as men and women rely on God to see to their needs. Exactly how much should a person give? That is an individual choice, and no formula is offered in the New Testament, but it brings to mind Paul's words when he told the Corinthians:

> "[6] Now this *I say*, he who sows sparingly will also reap sparingly, and he who sows bountifully will also reap bountifully. [7] Each one *must do* just as he has purposed in his heart, not grudgingly or under compulsion, for God loves a cheerful giver. [8] And God is able to make all grace abound to you, so that always having all sufficiency in everything, you may have an abundance for every good deed."
> (2 Corinthians 9: 6-8)

For those who are generous, God will provide. Indeed, he will provide all that is needed for one to fill a personal desire to be charitable. After all, what person of faith believes that God failed to meet the needs of the widow who gave her last coin to God? It is, however, a considerable leap of faith to begin giving sacrificially. It is personally challenging to give beyond what seems affordable or to give up something meaningful for the good of others. The cost of generosity must be weighed against the benefits of living life in a manner that pleases God. Generally, the spiritual benefit increases as the cost of giving increases. Jesus' lesson reflects the principle that one should never become complacent in giving and a believer must always challenge himself, refusing to be satisfied with his giving or reaching the point where he believes he has given *enough*.

It was Jesus' hope that his disciples would excel in generosity. That is the lesson of the last few verses. For instance, rather than seeking vengeance against those who seek to do them harm (an eye for an eye), Christ's followers are to be benevolent toward those who strike out against them, offering charity rather than seeking vengeance. People of faith are also to be generous toward those who attempt to steal from them, giving their coat as well as their shirt. Similarly, for those who seek help, the believer should offer more than they ask, *going the extra mile*. With these examples, Jesus was attempting to teach the disciples about the kind of unselfishness he hoped to see in those who wish to follow him.

Chapter Four

Matthew 6: 1-18

Pretentiousness

In the fifth chapter of Matthew, which was the topic of the first three chapters of this work, Jesus emphasized the high level of holiness and righteousness God expects from his followers. The high standards to which they were to hold themselves was juxtaposed, not against the unholy, unrighteous world, but against the religious activities prescribed in the law under which they had lived for so long. That is the comparison found in the many statements where Jesus quipped "you have heard…but I say." It was Jesus' goal to not only have his listeners understand God's view of what it means to live a holy and righteous life, but to desire that life.

A key word when considering what holiness/righteousness involves is the word *honesty*. The idea of honesty eclipses merely telling the truth. One can make statements that are true without being completely forthright. Language can be manipulated to one's own advantage, *allowing* others to infer what may ultimately lead to faulty conclusions. Honesty, on the other hand, refuses to participate in deception.

Deception does not always involve the spoken word. Sometimes it involves deceptive motivation. That is the idea behind purity of heart that was discussed earlier. It is a matter of being spiritually honest with oneself and with God.

The sixth chapter of Matthew, which is the second of three chapters that make up the *Sermon on the Mount*, begins with the word "Beware…" (v. 1). With this word, Jesus offered an ominous warning concerning righteous activity and heavenly rewards. Of what should his listeners beware? In a word, it is pretentiousness. Those who pretend to be righteous, putting on a show, so to speak, cannot honor God. All they really seek is recognition from men, which is merely a matter of pride. While they may very well achieve that goal, they should not expect to receive any appreciation from God.

This warning was offered in conjunction with Jesus' subsequent teaching concerning certain actions where one may find himself lauded by men, even if that was not the intent. His point was that a godly person will avoid performing good deeds in a manner that gains praise from other people. Instead, his motivation will be giving honor and glory to God.

Pretentious in Charity

The first activity Jesus addressed in this context is charitable giving (v. 2). The word he used is *alms* (Greek: *eleemosune*). Scripture differentiates between giving alms and putting money "…into the treasury" (Mark 12: 41). The treasury is a reference to money gifted to the work of the synagogue. The Jews were expected to contribute to the synagogue. However, alms represented money given to support the poor. Any money given as alms would have been considered above and beyond the normal call of duty. Still, the same principles of giving would apply to both, since Jesus recognized the two copper coins placed by the widow into the treasury as the *greater gift* (Mark 12: 42-43). In that instance, however, the focus was on the sacrifice of giving. Here, Jesus focused more on one's motivation for giving.

B. W. Johnson makes the case that Jesus' words in verse one are better represented by the NIV where it is stated, "Be careful not to practice your *righteousness* in front of others to be seen by them" (Matthew 6: 1, NIV – emphasis added). His argument is:

> The Common Version is wrong, and the Revision right, in using the word "righteousness." The Savior condemns ostentatious piety, and then he singles out three illustrations of his meaning. The Christian is not forbidden to practice righteousness before men, but to make it his object to be seen.[14]

Johnson's line of reasoning is that Jesus initially condemned performing any righteous activity specifically for the eyes of men and, in the ensuing verses, offered three examples where that principle would apply. Some Greek manuscripts use *eleemosune* (alms) in this

---

[14] Johnson, B. W., *The Peoples' New Testament with Explanatory Notes*, Gospel Light Publishing Company, Delight, AR

instance while others employ the word *dikaiosynēn* (righteousness). Johnson's point is that this word/translation better represents the essence of the text, which seems clear from the closing words of the previous chapter. In this verse, almsgiving is a general representation of righteous activity. According to *Zondervan Illustrated Bible Backgrounds Commentary Volume 1*:

'Acts of righteousness' are the public demonstration of one's piety, which in Judaism often centered on giving alms, praying, and fasting...[15]

Matthew's gospel was written from a Jewish perspective primarily to a Jewish audience. Almsgiving, prayer, and fasting were basic to the Jews' relationship with God. Jesus seems to make it clear in these verses that these righteous acts applied not only to the Jewish community, but to mankind in general. Consequently, they would be as much a part of man's relationship with God going forward as they had been in the past where the Jews were concerned. This suggests that these are *inherent* acts of righteousness rather than actions merely dictated through the Mosaic Law (e.g., animal sacrifices).

Charitable activity is often difficult to conceal from others. Someone else may well know what a person has done for others and, as a consequence, seek to recognize him publicly for his thoughtfulness. It is a tempting trap to simply allow praise to be heaped on oneself even if that was not the original intent of the charitable act. Unfortunately, this can be a slippery slope, which Jesus understood. Once praise is received, it can become addictive and ultimately lead one to begin performing charitable acts for the secondary, if not primary, purpose of receiving praise from other people.

The phrase "...do not sound a trumpet" (v. 2) sounds eerily like the English expression *blowing one's own horn*, and may well represent the origin of that idiom just as *going the extra mile* seems to have originated from Jesus' words in the previous chapter (5: 41). The fact that such commonplace proverb-like remarks likely developed from this single sermon demonstrate the depth and wisdom of Jesus' teaching.

---

[15] Arnold, Clinton E., Editor, *Zondervan Illustrated Bible Backgrounds Commentary, Volume 1*, Zondervan Publishing, Grand Rapids, 2002, p. 43.

Jesus used the trumpet reference as a criticism of a common practice that he considered objectionable. Certain pompous individuals were known for gathering the poor together by having a trumpet blown loudly for all to hear. At that sound, the poor, having been conditioned to respond to the trumpet much like dogs responded in Pavlov's experiment, would come scampering to receive whatever might be made available to them.

The problem Jesus was addressing was that, while the sound of the trumpet certainly attracted those who were destitute and in need of alms, placing them in a position where they could receive help, the real purpose was to attract the attention of the public toward the one who was providing for the poor. Thus, their almsgiving could be seen and praised by those in the community. Jesus considered this detestable and wanted his audience to recognize the vanity of those who would stoop to such a low level (using the poor) to be lauded by men. Clarke wrote about this custom in his well-known commentary, stating:

> Having something to distribute by way of alms, it is very probable they caused this to be published by blowing a *trumpet* or *horn*, under pretence of collecting the poor; though with no other design than to gratify their own ambition.[16]

Jesus followed these comments with a different perspective on humility in giving, telling the crowd that they should "...not let your left hand know what your right hand is doing" (v. 3) when it comes to charitable activity. This gives a sense of how private giving should be. Why should such giving be done "...in secret" (v. 4)? The reason this is necessary is that anything else dishonors God. When someone gives so that others will see, it is the individual, and not God, who is exalted.

On the other hand, when giving is done according to God's design – with a sense of humility (not allowing one's left hand to know what his right hand is doing) – God is honored. In other words, the godly person will be invisible where giving is concerned. When giving is between the individual who gives and the God in whose name he gives, that giving glorifies God. Additionally, Jesus made it clear that God, who sees all, rewards those who honor him in this way. Still, that reward should not be the motivation for charity, but merely a blessing

---

[16] Clarke, Adam, *The Adam Clarke Commentary*,
http://classic.studylight.org/com/acc/view.cgi?book=mt&chapter=006,
accessed 02/05/2017

one receives for doing what is right and doing it God's way; otherwise, giving is still about patting oneself on the back.

Pretentious in Prayer

The topic of charitable giving is followed by a lesson on prayer, which is the second of the three examples mentioned by Johnson. According to Jesus, prayer should not be a matter of vainglory. As an example, he offered a picture of those who "...stand and pray in the synagogues and on the street corners so that they may be seen by men" (v. 5), calling them hypocrites. Jesus showed great disdain for those who attempted to fake godliness. Hence, this is likely a reference to the Pharisees whom Jesus clearly saw as men who practiced false righteousness.

Throughout his ministry, Jesus often pointed to the Pharisees as a prime example of pseudo-faithfulness. They had come to consider themselves religiously superior, telling the Jews that following their teaching was the only way to truly serve God. Consequently, Jesus told his disciples that if they hoped to share in eternal heavenly rewards, their righteousness must surpass "...that of the scribes and Pharisees" (Matthew 5: 20).

Where one's prayer life is concerned, again Jesus' focus was on honesty and humility. Those who seek the praise of men will likely receive it. They will also need to learn to be satisfied in full with human praise since their reward from God will not be forthcoming. As with charitable giving, seeking praise from men is a prideful act and is a smack in the face of true godliness.

Two kinds of prayers are discussed by Jesus when considering the kind of prayer life that honors God. First of all, he addressed the topic of public prayer. There are times when people pray in groups of two or three or perhaps corporately. For instance, Matthew recorded Jesus' words when he spoke about his own presence when two or three gathered together in his name (Matthew 18: 19-20). Also, when God freed Peter from prison in Jerusalem, the apostle went to the house of Mark's mother, Mary, "where many were gathered together and were praying" (Acts 12: 12). Therefore, Scripture recognizes the value of praying together.

Public prayer was in view when Jesus ridiculed those who "...pray in the synagogues and on the street corners" (v. 5). While he did not prohibit public prayer, since it has its place, Jesus did show contempt toward vain public prayer where God was essentially excluded, recognizing that the words were spoken primarily for the benefit of those listening. When the goal is to say *pretty* public prayers so that men can appreciate how articulate, and perhaps how holy the speaker is, the very purpose of public prayer has been lost. In that vein, Jesus explained to the people that prayers that are intended to be heard primarily by men are anything but honorable. Indeed, they are anything but prayers.

Jesus offered some helpful instruction about corporate prayer that contrasts the misuse of synagogues and street corners mentioned above. As with other lessons in this sermon, the focus is on earnestness. He encouraged his audience to be genuine in their prayers, particularly where public prayer is concerned. They should not be like those who employ words of grandeur and/or vain phrases spoken repetitively for the sake of their listeners (v. 7). While such arrogance may grip the attention of one's fellowman, God will not be impressed. He knows one's requests before they are asked (v. 8), so he is more concerned with the sincerity of those requests.

God's preference is the private, sincere prayer that is a conversation between the believer and God. The more meaningful prayers are generally offered in private, Jesus telling the disciples to "...go into your inner room, close your door and pray to your Father who is in secret" (v. 6). If a person wishes to honor God with his/her prayer, the best way to do that is to pray privately where the affection that prayer affords can be fully realized by both the individual and God. This intimacy is at the very heart of one's walk with God and must be primary in a person's prayer life.

The Lord's Prayer

As a matter of further explanation about his teaching on prayer, Jesus offered his disciples an example of the kind of prayer God deems appropriate. In what has come to be known as the Lord's Prayer, the character of an honorable prayer is thoughtfully displayed. The Lord's Prayer is not a prayer people are commanded to pray either as individuals or in unison. That was not Jesus' purpose. His goal was to provide his listeners with an understanding of the kinds of things one might address in prayer offered up to the Father.

In the prayer example Jesus offered the disciples, several things are noticeable. First of all, approaching God with a sense of reverence is critical for someone who wishes to have his ear. Therefore, Jesus began with the manner in which one should approach such a conversation with God. His first words were, "Our Father who is in heaven, Hallowed be Your name" (v. 9). The word *hallowed* means *holy*, *sacred*, or *divine*. In other words, this is a matter of giving God his due and recognizing him for who he is – reverently addressing him as the Almighty.

This approach very much harmonizes with the words of the prophet, Micah who, in describing God's expectations of mankind, stated that men are to "…walk humbly with your God" (Micah 6: 8). A humble approach toward the Father will go far in gaining God's attention. It is safe to say that God hears every prayer that is prayed by men, since he is all-knowing. However, while God may hear all prayers, it does not mean that he listens to all prayers. Jesus has already indicated the ineffectiveness of duplicitous prayers offered as a matter of vanity (v. 5). It is the prayer of the righteous – those who fully accept that they have no real standing to demand anything from God – that are most effective (James 5: 16).

Thoughtful, genuine prayers involve kingdom thoughts. That is to say, the person offering the prayer always places the kingdom of God first. Hence, Jesus stated, "Your kingdom come. Your will be done, On earth as it is in heaven" (v. 10). The person who seeks to walk with God places the good of the kingdom before the wants and needs of himself and others.

It is clear from Jesus' words that prayer is not about the will of the individual believer, but about God's will. Prayer often involves approaching God with requests for sustained/improved health for self and/or others, or that he might deliver someone from contrary circumstances, or that he would provide the believer with strength to endure the earthly trials men face. These are all reasonable, understandable requests. Yet, the will of the person who prays earnestly will submit humbly to the will of God knowing that he will do what is best in answer to that prayer.

Jesus understands that men have physical needs and asking God to provide for such needs is not contradictory to Jesus' teaching about prayer. Thus, he includes "Give us this day our daily bread" (v. 11). God has made it clear that mankind is his most important physical creation. Therefore, he is willing and ready to provide what is necessary and good for man to live according to his ways, a topic Jesus addresses in greater depth later in this chapter (vv. 25-34).

The statement, "And forgive us our debts, as we also have forgiven our debtors" (v. 12), seems to combine two distinct godly principles.

First of all, an individual should seek forgiveness for his sins. This is a principle that is taught a number of times in God's Word. Second, however, there seems to be a sense that it is not only good to ask God to forgive sins, but to hold the believer accountable when it comes to forgiving others. Asking him to forgive "as we also have forgiven our debtors," is an example of the believer reaching out to God and seeking his assistance in helping him overcome human weakness that might prevent him from forgiving others.

With the words, "And do not lead us into temptation…" (v. 13), Jesus was not suggesting that God would, either intentionally or unintentionally, entice one to sin. This would be contrary to what is known of God from Scripture in that he "…cannot be tempted by evil, and He Himself does not tempt anyone" (James 1: 13). Scholars do not fully see eye to eye about the meaning of the Greek *petrasmos* (temptation) in the verse, since it is often, both within and without Scripture, used to identify the testing of an individual (cf. Matthew 4: 1-12). However, that meaning should not be applied too hastily here, since God does test people. Indeed, he may well test others as he tested Abraham (cf. Genesis 22: 1-12). Such testing can strengthen one's faith (cf. Revelation 2: 9-10). Consequently, it seems incompatible with biblical principles that the believer would ask God to keep him from being tested.

Another sense in which this word is used is the idea of *falling prey to*, or *succumbing to* the temptations presented by the world (cf. Mark 14: 38; Galatians 6: 1). This is certainly a reasonable approach to this word in the current passage. Who would not want God's help in avoiding sin? Therefore, this is a practical explanation of Jesus' use of this word. Still, there is another, perhaps even more reasonable possibility.

When someone chooses to follow Jesus, that person also chooses to walk with God. This is the primary theme of the Apostle John's first epistle where he calls it *walking in the light where God is the light* (1 John 1: 7). The idea is not that one simply fellowships with God, but that he allows God to choose the path he will follow. It stands to reason, then, that if God is one's guide, it is a reasonable request to ask him to keep the believer close to him in order to avoid the pitfalls of temptation. It would be much like asking someone who knows their locations to help others avoid the mines in a minefield. God does, with his Word, provide direction that will help his children avoid temptation (cf. Philippians 4: 8). Therefore, this final explanation may well be the most reasonable of all for Jesus' thoughts.

In complement with the notion of avoiding temptation, Jesus suggested that it is reasonable and good to ask God to "…deliver us from evil" (v. 13). A few possibilities exist concerning Jesus' thoughts. First of all, the phrase "deliver us" could be a reference to prevention or preservation. In other words, it could be a request that God *spare us from evil*. It could also involve the idea of rescuing the believer from evil, or sins to which he has already succumbed. Either or both of these might offer an acceptable interpretation.

That having been said, how one reads the term "deliver us" may well depend on how the word *evil* is understood. Some scholars believe the word is being used in the generic sense of ungodliness or sin. Others insist that the Greek form of *tou penērou* that appears here could be read as masculine and, as such, have determined that it is likely a reference, not to *evil*, but to *the evil one*, or Satan. Certain English translations (ASV, CEB, NIV, and NRSV) prefer this rendering. The Greek *apo*, translated here as *from*, also generally suggests rescue or protection from a person rather than a thing or a concept, which strengthens that argument. Therefore, it is likely that Jesus was suggesting that it would be wise to offer prayer that God would provide protection or rescue from the clutches of Satan.

The closing of the Lord's Prayer, also called the doxology, where Jesus stated, "For Yours is the kingdom and the power and the glory forever. Amen" (v. 13), is actually lacking in the oldest known Greek manuscripts. For this reason, many scholars believe it was a late addition to the text. This view is further supported by the fact that, in the numerous manuscripts where it appears, a wide variety of versions have been discovered.

Despite the fact that this is likely a late addition to the text, few argue about its worth. The idea behind this statement is that of perspective. While the prayer enjoins three common facets of prayer (i.e., praise, petition, and glory/honor), these words help the reader recognize the value of the earlier remark, "Your will be done" (v. 10), which is at the heart of the doxology. This helps keep in perspective the idea that petitions are not commands and that God is ultimately in control. After all, men are the created beings, and he is the uncreated. Still, the heart that seeks God is also noticed by him, so petitions of a believer should never be considered meaningless. According to the prayer example given by Jesus, men should not hesitate to petition

God. A quality prayer life can only serve to strengthen one's walk of faith.

Forgiveness

Following the Lord's Prayer, Jesus offered some additional insight into the words of that prayer (v. 14). Specifically, he discussed verse twelve and the topic of forgiveness. In that verse he stated, "...forgive us our debts, as we also have forgiven our debtors." He evidently believed the balance of the prayer spoke for itself but wanted to make sure the disciples did not overlook the point of this particular verse.

His emphasis in this verse is on forgiveness. However, it is not just about mankind receiving forgiveness from God for sinful transgressions. God wants people to not only be forgiven, but to be forgiving. There is, of course, a cost for forgiveness. When an individual forgives another, what he is really saying is that he will take the cost of their transgression upon himself and off of them, much like Jesus did on the cross. For instance, when someone forgives a monetary debt, the one who forgives is, in essence, removing the cost of that debt from the shoulders of the debtor and placing it upon his own shoulders. That is to say he is paying the debt himself. When someone does harm to another, whether it is physical harm, reputation, or some other matter, and the injured party chooses to forgive, he is accepting the cost of that wrong rather than making the wrongdoer pay for it. The person who truly seeks to be like Jesus will, indeed, show mercy through forgiveness.

So important is forgiveness that Jesus linked the believer's forgiveness of others and God's forgiveness of the believer. In other words, if one is unforgiving where others are concerned, that person has no reason to expect forgiveness from God (v. 15). That is the biblical principle that can be drawn from the parable of the unmerciful servant (Matthew 18: 21-35). If a person truly wishes to walk with God, forgiveness must become part of his character. That is the lesson Jesus had in view.

Pretentious in Fasting

Fasting is a sensitive topic for most people and serves as Jesus' third example concerning religious hypocrisy. The sensitivity that is linked to fasting is found in the fact that, with very few exceptions, people love food. Fasting is an interesting individual biblical study in itself, but Jesus briefly touched on it here. The general purpose of fasting is to help a person focus on the spiritual rather than the physical aspects of life. Old Testament national fasts under the Mosaic Law were commanded for specific purposes such as remembrance (Zechariah 7: 3-5). Group fasts were generally done to foster a sense of humility and were often done in conjunction with repentance as the Israelites sought forgiveness for their sins (Nehemiah 9: 1-2). Other times fasting was employed to lay a particular petition before God (cf. 2 Samuel 1: 12).

In the New Testament, fasting is presented as a matter of Christian discipline and spiritual fitness. Many of the same reasons people fasted in the Old Testament are repeated in the New Testament. Paul fasted out of anguish (Acts 9: 9) when he realized he had been wrong about Jesus. He fasted while seeking direction for his life and evidently forgiveness for the error of his ways. Also, the church in Antioch fasted and prayed concerning Paul and Barnabas prior to sending them on Paul's first missionary journey (Acts 13: 3).

Rather than focusing on the purpose and/or benefits of fasting, in these verses, Jesus emphasized one's attitude in fasting. He began by warning against fasting for the wrong reasons. If someone chooses to fast, he should go about his daily activities *as though he is not fasting.* There should be nothing about the fast that in any way draws attention to the one who is fasting (v. 16). If a person *shows off* in his fasting, it would be comparable to selfishly giving (vv. 2-3) or praying (vv. 5-6) merely to be honored by men rather than God. For those who fast to gain accolades from men, that is their reward. However, the fast serves no spiritual purpose and delivers no spiritual benefit.

The fast affords a great opportunity in those quiet moments when one is alone with God during the fast. Prayer and fasting are complementary and work in harmony. The prayers offered during a fast tend to be more intense and more focused than others. God recognizes and rewards this extra effort (v. 18). To him, it means the one who is fasting appreciates, and takes seriously, his/her walk with God.

Greater appreciation of God's Word can also be experienced during a fast. Studying can become more meaningful and keenness of understanding enhanced when fasting. Each word of Scripture can take on greater significance, and insight into its meaning can be improved through the focus that fasting offers. Drawing the attention of men can weaken the intensity of the fast and diminish these benefits so that the fast will not serve its intended purpose.

Chapter Five

Matthew 6: 19-24

Spiritual Investing

Jesus quickly moved from the topic of fasting to that of treasure. While he spoke only two sentences on the subject, they are powerful verses. He instructed the disciples to "...not store up for yourselves treasures on earth, where moth and rust destroy, and where thieves break in and steal" (v. 19). The Greek *thesaurizete*, which is translated "store up," speaks to the idea of investing. The literal translation is *place into tomorrow*. He followed this with the advice, "...store up for yourselves treasures in heaven, where neither moth nor rust destroys, and where thieves do not break in or steal" (v. 20).

According to Jesus, investments should be considered carefully, recognizing that the return on one's spiritual investment far outweighs any return he could expect from earthly investments. Upon death, no one will take his earthly treasures with him. Any benefit a person receives from those investments will be limited to this earthly existence. Additionally, earthly possessions can be subject to one's surroundings. They could be stolen, lost during economic misfortune, or destroyed in a physical disaster (storm, fire, etc.).

Spiritual investments, however, provide benefits beyond this life. Ironically, when one charitably gives away a possession as a matter of spiritual investment, that possession can no longer be stolen from him. It cannot be lost during economic heartbreak or physical disaster. Also, the spiritual return that one receives cannot be measured in human terms. Thus, Jesus is talking about his disciples investing in their spiritual future.

The focus in these verses is on one's sense of priorities. Concentrating on the benefits one might receive in this current physical state demonstrates a lack of spiritual perspective. Concentrating on selfish desires for a few decades of life in these earthly shells, while ignoring the opportunities to make eternal spiritual investments, shows little respect for the teachings of Christ as well as godliness in general.

Jesus closed his thoughts on investment with what is arguably one of the most cited phrases in all of Scripture stating, "…for where your treasure is, there your heart will be also" (v. 21). This is as profound a statement as can be found in the writings on earth, but what was his meaning? He was saying that what a person does with his/her money is the single greatest indicator concerning that person's priorities. It demonstrates what is most important to an individual. It reveals to others and to God where that person's heart is.

A godly person is a giving person. It is inherent in the Christian character to be charitable. When Jesus met with the rich young ruler (Matthew 19: 16-22) and suggested that the man should use his wealth to provide for the poor, the young man was disheartened. He could not part with his wealth. That is where his heart was. Retaining his wealth meant more to him than any spiritual benefit he might reap by giving it away. He chose to *place into tomorrow* only what could benefit him in this life.

In these verses, Jesus speaks expressly about mankind's relationship with money, or treasure; and people certainly have an affinity for cash. It can bring out the best or the worst in an individual. However, it seems reasonable to extrapolate his teaching to the greater idea of what one does with his/her earthly resources in general. Money, it seems, is intended to be representative of all earthly possessions and how they are used. What other resources are available that could be related to these teachings?

The first resource that comes to mind is time. Everyone possesses time and it can be spent in much the same way money is spent. It can be used selfishly or generously. How is it spent? Is it used for personal benefit/gratification or is it used to benefit others? Certainly, some of one's time is used to earn money to provide for self and family, which is one thing that makes time so precious. In truth, it is the fact that money represents one's time that gives money its worth. However, time is also spent on things other than earning money, and like money, time can be used to honor or dishonor God.

An individual's life is filled with assorted relationships. It involves family, friends, co-workers, etc., and these relationships are precious possessions. They are a valuable resource, but how are they used? Is God honored in those relationships or is he absent from them? Perhaps certain relationships are best abandoned as a matter of honoring God (cf. 1 Corinthians 15: 33). These questions are equally relevant to Jesus' comments about a believer's resources.

When Jesus spoke of treasure, it stands to reason that he had in view a person's total worth. Jesus was not short-sighted, and it would be foolish to believe that, when speaking of wealth, he was limiting the idea strictly to money or other valuable physical possessions. Responding to the rich young ruler, Jesus not only told him that he should sell his possessions and offer the proceeds to the poor, but that he should surrender his valuable resource of time, telling the young man, "…and come, follow me" (Matthew 19: 21).

It is important to avoid reading into Jesus' words things he did not say. For instance, earthly possessions should not be seen as inherently evil. Believers must recognize that possessions are not only good, but they are God-given. They are a resource that can be used by the faithful to serve him by doing that which is good (Ephesians 2: 10). As such, their worth must be respected, and they should be used to honor God.

It is a fallacy to presume that it is God's plan for believers to possess great wealth, as some men teach. Nothing about Jesus' teachings could lead the reasonable, spiritually minded person to this conclusion. Some believers may well be wealthy, but others may not be. Rest assured that the distinction is not grounded in their measure of faith. Who could doubt the faith of the widow who gave up her final two coins to God? (Luke 21: 1-4).

While some like to preach health and wealth religion, Scripture teaches that the faithful will be generous, not stingy with their possessions. Also, believers may experience financial and/or health challenges just as unbelievers. Earlier in this very sermon, Jesus said, "He causes His sun to rise on *the* evil and *the* good, and sends rain on *the* righteous and *the* unrighteous" (Matthew 5: 45). That lesson seems plain enough.

Light and Dark

Having discussed the connection between financial resources and one's relationship with God, Jesus appears to move on, touching on the idea of light and dark. Some may consider this a strange transition since it comes on the heels of a discussion about spiritual investment and the wise use of one's resources. However, most are unaware of the subtle Greek word play of the passage. Therefore, they do not make the connection as it is intended. It is this subtlety that not only provides the connection but makes it a reasonable follow-up to Jesus' thoughts just given.

The Greek *haplous*, which the NASB translates as *clear* in the current setting, is often seen as denoting generosity. It is reminiscent of the relationship between *beneficial*, a word that could be written in place of *clear* in this instance, and the idea of *benevolence*, which has charitable implications. The NIV translates *haplous* as *good* in this setting, which is another way of saying *beneficial*. In other words, Jesus is speaking, in his own way, of that which benefits spiritually and that which does not, much like what he was saying about spiritual investment.

In this case, Jesus was speaking of a *good* (clear or beneficial) eye and a bad eye. The *New Bible Commentary* states that "the bad eye of *verse 23* is a metaphor for stinginess and jealousy."[17] This speaks to the charitable vs. selfish relationship with possessions that was just discussed. Jesus would have been aware of this connection, which is probably why he chose these specific words.

Light is often used figuratively in Scripture to reflect God or godliness. Even earlier in this very sermon, believers are called "...the light of the world" (Matthew 5: 14). Countless other passages also reference light in a similar manner. It is also used as a figure of clarity and/or understanding (John 3: 21; Romans 2: 19). Light is a primary focus in both the gospel of John and in his first epistle, where *walking in the light* (godliness and understanding) is depicted as a way of life for those who love God.

Here Jesus discussed light in spiritual terms. He called the eye "...the lamp of the body" (v. 22). It does not emit light as a lamp does but is a lamp *into* the body. Eyes collect light so that people can comprehend their surroundings and know how to interact with them. Thus, the eye is the source of light for one's mind. Similarly, everyone has a spiritual eye, which is what Jesus was discussing here. It does not collect physical, but spiritual light (information) so that informed spiritual decisions can be made much like the physical eye allows for reasonable decision-making where the physical world is concerned.

When someone has poor eyesight, it is difficult to navigate physical surroundings, since so many choices rely on knowledge that is provided through sight. It is challenging to read, drive a car, or react to moving objects. Similarly, someone whose eyes are not spiritually

---

[17] Wenham, G. J., Motyer, J. A., Carson, D. A., and France, R. T., editors, *New Bible Commentary*,Intervarsity Press, Nortingham, England, 1994, p. 913

opened, taking in worthwhile spiritual information, will find it difficult to comprehend and navigate things spiritual.

It is generally true that someone who has poor physical eyesight has not chosen to be disadvantaged in this way. This is one of the greatest differences between those who are physically blind and those who are spiritually blind. The spiritually blind generally choose that condition, failing and/or refusing to look into spiritual things. Therefore, they are "full of darkness," spiritually speaking. James discusses this willing blindness, comparing the person who ignores godly instruction to a man "[23] ...who looks at his natural face in a mirror; [24] for *once* he has looked at himself and gone away, he has immediately forgotten what kind of person he was" (James 1: 23-24). In other words, what he has seen with his eyes is meaningless to him. It is as though he never looked in the mirror.

Jesus closed this section by blending his teaching concerning giving with his teaching about light. These teachings are really lessons about one's heart. The person who loves God is a giving person. He is also religiously perceptive, constantly using his spiritual vision to seek the ways of God. Jesus summarized his discussion about one's heart with an explanation that "No one can serve two masters" (v. 24). The person who is selfish (uncharitable) does not recognize God as his master. Also, one who chooses spiritual blindness does not serve God. Such a person serves someone else and, according to Jesus, it is not possible to serve God and serve someone else.

With these words, Jesus figuratively personified wealth and darkness as rival gods who compete for one's attention/service. Either God is served fully and without reservation, or he is not served at all. In this particular case, he stated that one "...cannot serve God and wealth" (v. 24). While this statement seems to be more closely associated with Jesus' remark about treasure (v. 19), it also complements his comment about light (vv. 22-23) since it is usually the things of this world that seem to blind men when it comes to seeking God or addressing spiritual well-being.

Chapter Six

Matthew 6: 25-34

Trusting in God for the Basics

When men devote themselves to wealth, or earthly possessions, there is an undeniable consequence in that they also become dependent on earthly wealth and possessions. These possessions become a source of comfort and security. The problem with this is that earthly wealth cannot provide the kind of security men truly desire. It is futile to rely on earthly possessions for security since 1) life is fragile and can be snatched away quickly and 2) life consists of much more than physical attributes or comforts. The godly person will learn to overcome reliance on the physical. This is why Jesus encouraged his disciples to fast (v. 16), be charitable (v. 19), and seek spiritual understanding by refusing to be spiritually blind (v. 22).

Jesus offered his disciples a recipe for happiness. He explained why they should not be concerned with even their physical needs. It is significant that Jesus did not, in these verses, speak of human excesses. He was not concerned with royal feasts, extravagant clothing, palaces, or wealth with which one might fill his every human desire. Instead, he spoke of food, clothing, and shelter in terms of basic human needs.

According to Jesus, if a person wishes to know security, he must rest in the comfort of knowing that God is a loving father. Therefore, there is no need to worry about daily essentials. God will provide for those who trust in him. This can be difficult, of course, since it is much easier to trust in that which is seen than that which is unseen, but that is the test of faith with which God has challenged his children.

As with all of Scripture, it is important to avoid reading into the passage something that is not there. The King James reads, "Take no thought for your life, what ye shall eat, or what ye shall drink; nor yet for your body, what ye shall put on" (v. 25). However, Jesus was not suggesting that a believer should not be concerned *at all* with life's essentials. What he was saying is that such things should not be given *undue* consideration. It is important for God's faithful to have a proper perspective when it comes to items like food, clothing, and shelter. The Greek *merimnate* means believers are not to *worry* or *be anxious* about such things. The idea this word conveys is probably best expressed with the archaic English word *solicitous*, which is not used much today, but suggests imagery of *excessive attention*. Some translations employ the term *worry* in this setting (NASB, NIV, RSV) while others offer the word *anxious* as an appropriate translation (ASV, NRSV).

Jesus was not saying that God will instantly and miraculously deliver clothes to people's closets or place food on the table. Believers are to work to provide for self and family. This biblical principal (cf. Proverbs 10: 1-16) does not contradict Jesus' claim that God will provide, but complements it. He can make the work performed by the hands of the righteous more productive than it might otherwise have been (cf. Psalm 1: 1-3). Thus, he uses the opportunity to work as a means to provide...work that, by its very nature, makes for more godly individuals since God is naturally an avid worker.

The Lord furthered his point by providing some analogies for the disciples. He suggested that they should be no more concerned with their basic needs than they should be concerned about their own length of life. Not one of them could, through solicitude, "add a *single* hour to his life" (v. 27). Thus, it would be futile for them to dwell on the topic. This same futility applies to these other areas.

Jesus mentioned how God cares for "...the birds of the air" (v. 26) and "...the lilies of the field" (v. 28). They are gloriously arrayed and never lack what they need. The beauty of the lilies even surpasses the splendor of the clothing of King Solomon (v. 29) who was one of the wealthiest men to ever live.

The grass of the field, according to Jesus, "...is *alive* today and tomorrow is thrown into the furnace" (v. 30). In other words, it is a mere weed that grows and dies and grows again. Its life is fleeting and insignificant. Grass was not formed in the image of God as was man, yet God cares for it and adorns it beautifully. How much more, then, could they expect God to care for mankind, who was formed in his image?

Jesus explained the futility of worrying about things like food and clothing, calling the people "You of little faith" (v. 30). He exhorted them to trust in God more. After all, they were much more important to God than birds and flowers. Therefore, they should not be unduly concerned with what they would eat, or drink, or wear.

The great irony is that, while Jesus may well have been talking to the larger crowd at this time in the sermon, it would be his closest disciples who, later in Jesus' ministry, were solicitous when it came to food. When Jesus fed the five thousand (Matthew 14: 15-21), and later when he fed the four thousand (Matthew 15: 32-38), the disciples seemed, early on, to be dispirited about their own lack of food. Later they again despaired over having no bread to eat (Matthew 16: 5-12), having forgotten how handy Jesus was at providing. They had also evidently forgotten this lesson from the *Sermon on the Mount* concerning such things.

Where faith comes into play is the recognition that those who live godly lives need not worry about whether they will have jobs or where their next meal will come from, etc. In other words, believers need not hoard for themselves in order to care for themselves. They can be the generous, selfless people God wants them to be.

The person of faith need not worry about food, drink, clothing, or shelter because the person of faith is not of this world, *per se*. Thus, his/her thoughts are not about food and clothing. They are spiritual thoughts as the kingdom of God is of primary focus. Concerns over physical needs are secondary.

Paul told the Philippians that he had learned to be content in all circumstances (Philippians 4: 11-12). There is nothing wrong with having a nice house or a new car. However, the person who places excess emphasis on these things, and cannot be content without them, is a person who has lost touch with God. They fear losing their *possessions*.

The Christian's emphasis should be on seeking the kingdom of God. This should be his highest priority. When that happens, cars and houses become less important. The believer's focus should be on what he can do for others and not what he can accumulate for himself. That does not mean that God will not provide the believer with a quality physical life. It simply means that if a child of God must go without, it will simply serve to strengthen his faith. That is what happens when people learn to be content in all circumstances. Consequently, believers need not worry about tomorrow (v. 34). If one's faith rests in Jesus, there is nothing that can happen that will destroy him since his faith is not in the physical, but in the spiritual.

Chapter Seven

Matthew 7: 1-6

Judging Others

There are those who love to turn to the first verse of the seventh chapter of Matthew in an attempt to avoid receiving judgment from others for their actions. The claim is that no one is allowed to judge their actions because the bible clearly states, "Do not judge so that you will not be judged" (v. 1). However, the idea behind this passage is not quite that simple. Jesus was not prohibiting the passing of judgment. If that was the case, it would conflict with considerable instruction found elsewhere in Scripture. For instance, the apostle John instructed the believers to "...judge with righteous judgment" (John 7: 24). At times it is necessary to judge whether someone is being truthful, particularly about the gospel message (Galatians 1: 8-9; Philippians 3: 2). John also wrote that believers are to "...test the spirits" (1 John 4: 1). Therefore, Christians are often called upon to make moral and righteous judgments.

The church is also called to make judgments about the actions of her members. Paul discussed with the Corinthians the need to address immorality in the church. He told the believers there "...not to associate with any so-called brother if he is an immoral person, or covetous, or an idolater, or a reviler, or a drunkard, or a swindler—not even to eat with such a one" (1 Corinthians 5: 11). With these things in view, it is probably fair to say that Jesus was not, with the words "Do not judge...," commanding believers to completely avoid judging the deeds of other people.

Perhaps a better way to explain what Jesus intended is to say that people ought to avoid *being judgmental*. In other words, he was not only talking about the *equity* of the judgments, but also the *spirit* (attitude) with which those judgments are made. It is easy to find fault with the seemingly foolish actions and decisions of others. Such is the source of much idle gossip. It is not only easy, but it can be a bit satisfying to weigh the foolish decisions of others against one's own obviously wise and godly choices. It is a prideful matter to do so and can only serve to drive others away. It will drive them away from the person who insists on being judgmental and, if he/she claims to be a representative of Jesus, it may well drive them away from him, too.

When Jesus told the disciples not to judge, he was explaining to them how judgment works from God's perspective. The Greek word that is translated judge (*krinō*) means *to judge, to condemn,* or *to discern,* so the concept is broad. However, what Jesus was telling the disciples here is that they will be judged by God with the same kind of scale they use to judge others (v. 2).

One's own manner of judgment toward others will be used in reverse. If one is harsh and unreasonable (hateful or spiteful) when judging the activities of others, insisting on the strictest discipline available for a seemingly small indiscretion, that person can expect his/her own activities to be judged in like manner. However, if one's judgment is bathed in compassion and mercy, seeking to reconcile those who have erred and even assisting those who need help to right their path, comparable judgment from God can be expected. *Commentary Critical and Explanatory of the Whole Bible* states, "Unkind judgment of others will be judicially returned upon ourselves, in the day when God shall judge the secrets of men by Jesus Christ."[18]

It is also possible, and perhaps likely, that Jesus was alluding to the idea that no one should presume to judge others on God's behalf, or as his surrogates. Ultimate judgment of men's actions (i.e., eternal judgment) belongs to God rather than men. The Christian's role in judging others should be limited to helping guide them in their walk with God.

For the believer, it can feel awkward to be placed in the difficult position of having to make judgments about the actions and decisions of others. While believers may at times find themselves in the unenviable position of having to weigh another person's actions – primarily brothers and sisters in Christ – it is important to keep that role in perspective. It is imperative that judgment must always be bathed in love and mercy and guided by prayer. This will help relieve

---

[18] Jamieson, Robert, Fausset, A. R., Brown, David, *Commentary Critical and Explanatory of the Whole Bible*,
https://www.studylight.org/commentaries/jfb/matthew-7.html,
accessed April 4, 2017

the burden of judging since any judgment rendered will be grounded in godliness. It will also assure that God will in turn judge this same believer as lovingly and mercifully as his righteousness will allow.

Hypocrisy in Judging

Jesus noted the hypocrisy that is often involved when it comes to judging others, offering a hyperbolic analogy to which he believed his listeners could relate. In this case, he explained judgment in terms of a speck and a log. According to Jesus, one might easily notice a small fleck (from the Greek *karphos* meaning *mote* or *speck of dust*) in his brother's eye while failing to recognize the full-sized log (from the Greek *dokon* meaning *timber* or *beam*) protruding out of his own eye (v. 3).

The speck and the log represent human flaws or poor human decision-making. It is safe to say that the person who has a log in his own eye is using unbalanced scales by ignoring his own faults while condemning another whose faults are miniscule by comparison. He is not putting a thumb on the scale; he is putting a boulder on the scale. This kind of person is eager to rebuke others but rejects the notion that anyone else is suited to judge him. In God's eyes, one who judges with this kind of spiritual vanity effectively surrenders his own standing to pass judgment on anyone else.

The person condemning his brother for the speck in his eye either blindly fails to see, or blatantly refuses to recognize, his own flaws that are exponentially greater. Usually, it is the latter. This speaks volumes about the arrogance of this kind of person. Jesus unflinchingly described that person as a hypocrite, a term he used to describe disingenuousness earlier in his sermon. It is the same term he applied to the Pharisees repeatedly during his encounters with them (cf. Matthew 15: 1-9; 22: 15-22; 23: 13-29).

Jesus has no respect for hypocrites and despises insincerity, particularly from those who claim to represent him. It seems safe to say that it would not be a good thing to be seen as a hypocrite in his eyes. For this reason, rather than taking on the likeness of what Jesus considers a hypocrite, it would be wise to always do some self-reflection before judging others for their actions or decisions. One should always take the time, using a balanced scale, to self-evaluate before criticizing a brother for the speck in his eye (v. 5).

Pearls before Swine

It becomes clear that verse one does not prohibit all judgment since Jesus follows his thoughts about not being judgmental of others with a prime example of an area where judgment is necessary. He stated, "Do not give what is holy to dogs, and do not throw your pearls before swine, or they will trample them under their feet, and turn and tear you to pieces" (v. 6). However, this verse puts the believer in the unenviable position of deciding who is a *dog* or who is a *swine*.

What is the meaning of this phrase? Jesus had just warned the disciples about the danger of being too judgmental. However, it appears he did not want this to result in complacency. Just as Paul warned the Corinthians to distance themselves from those who were immoral, Jesus did not want these disciples to fail to recognize evildoers simply because they did not want to be seen as the person with a log in his eye.

What is the pearl in this setting? In many of his parables, Jesus pointed to the kingdom of heaven (with an allusion to the gospel message through which the kingdom is made available to men) as that which is most precious. Jesus told his disciples, "The kingdom of heaven is like treasure hidden in a field..." (Matthew 13: 44). He followed this with the statement "...the kingdom of heaven is like a merchant looking for fine pearls..." (Matthew 13: 45).

It is easy to see how the idea of the kingdom of heaven, or the gospel message, fits into Jesus' thoughts; but who are the swine and the dogs? Who is it with whom the faithful should not share the gospel? Everyone is a sinner, so no one is really worthy of the kingdom. Why, then, would Jesus say, "Do not give what is holy to dogs, and do not throw your pearls before swine, or they will trample them under their feet, and turn and tear you to pieces" (v. 6)?

It is of note that dogs and swine were unclean animals where the Jews were concerned. Additionally, for some reason dogs were particularly reviled by the Jews as can be seen in the Old Testament where they were often depicted in figurative language as loathsome creatures (cf. Job 30: 1; Psalm 22: 16). This explains why the Jews liked to use the term *dog* as a signature term for Gentiles (cf. Matthew 15: 26).

In similar fashion in the Old Testament, swine were often used in figurative language to represent a less appealing nature. For instance, Solomon wrote:

As a ring of gold in a swine's snout
So is a beautiful woman who lacks discretion. (Proverbs 11: 22).

Consequently, when Jesus spoke of dogs and swine, the reference had more significance to the Jewish people than it would have for those who live in the modern world where a dog is often referred to as man's best friend.

While no one is worthy of the kingdom, believers are compelled to share the good news with everyone. Jesus' point is that there are those who, learning of the kingdom, will seek to trample under foot the opportunity God has offered. The dogs and swine seem to represent those mentioned by the apostle Peter in his second epistle where he penned the following.

[17] These are springs without water and mists driven by a storm, for whom the black darkness has been reserved. [18] For speaking out arrogant *words* of vanity they entice by fleshly desires, by sensuality, those who barely escape from the ones who live in error, [19] promising them freedom while they themselves are slaves of corruption; for by what a man is overcome, by this he is enslaved. [20] For if, after they have escaped the defilements of the world by the knowledge of the Lord and Savior Jesus Christ, they are again entangled in them and are overcome, the last state has become worse for them than the first. [21] For it would be better for them not to have known the way of righteousness, than having known it, to turn away from the holy commandment handed on to them. [22] It has happened to them according to the true proverb, 'A DOG RETURNS TO ITS OWN VOMIT,' and, 'A sow, after washing, *returns* to wallowing in the mire.' (2 Peter 2: 17-22)

Peter's citation about the dog who returns to his vomit (v. 22) comes from Proverbs where Solomon wrote about how foolish people make the same mistakes repeatedly. According to the apostle, these people are worse off than before they heard the gospel since having heard it, they again become entangled in corruption and the ways of the world, often taking others with them. This could include those the apostles warned against who pervert the gospel, thus leading people astray (cf. Philippians 3: 2; Colossians 2: 8; 1 Timothy 6: 3-5). They are represented here with the words "...springs without water and mists driven by a storm" (2 Peter 2: 17). They claim to be godly teachers, but their teaching has no substance. Others, having turned from godliness will, with malice, not only thrive in their corruption, but seek to destroy the faith of those who believe (cf. 1 John 2: 26).

The believer's time is better spent sharing the gospel with those who, even if not receptive, are not spiteful toward God and Christianity. Those who turn away after having "...escaped the defilements of the world by the knowledge of the Lord and Savior Jesus Christ" (2 Peter 2: 20) and refuse to be reconciled to God, should be rebuked and rejected, having foolishly wasted the opportunity afforded them in Christ.

Chapter Eight

Matthew 7: 7-12

God and Prayer

Men often approach prayer as a matter of petitioning God. In this particular segment, that petitioning of God seems to be the focus of Jesus' teaching. Earlier in the *Sermon on the Mount*, as Jesus taught the disciples about prayer, he encouraged them to ask God to provide for their needs (Matthew 6: 9-13). This is something God wants his children to do, and these verses speak to that part of one's relationship with him.

According to Jesus, the believer needs only ask of God and, believing, will receive (vv. 8-9). However, the verse actually says more than this. Jesus refers to three distinct elements that come into play when earnestly seeking God's help. Ellicott describes them as follows:

> The three words imply distinct degrees of intensity. There is the 'asking' in the spoken words of prayer, the 'seeking' in the efforts and labours which are acted prayers, the 'knocking' at the gate with the urgent importunity which claims admission into our Father's house.[19]

In this passage, Jesus compared the believer's relationship with God to the relationship between a father and his son. This is an analogy that is repeated consistently throughout Scripture (Matthew 5: 9; Acts 17: 29; Romans 8: 16; Galatians 3: 26). His point was that, if a son asks his father for a loaf of bread, his father would not give him a stone instead (v. 9). No good man would mock his son in such a callous fashion. Similarly, if a son asks his father for a fish,

---

[19] Ellicott, *Ellicott's Commentary for English Readers*, https://www.studylight.org/commentaries/ebc/matthew-7.html, accessed 03/21/2017.

his father would not give him a snake (v. 10). In that same sense, a believer can expect to receive good things from his/her spiritual father (v. 11).

This raises the question: *Why do people not always receive from God exactly what has been requested?* People die despite the fact that others pray for them to live. There is still hunger and suffering in the world notwithstanding the countless prayers seeking relief for those in need. The number of seemingly unanswered prayers stretches far beyond what most can imagine. How, then, can this be reconciled with Jesus' words stating that all one needs to do is ask?

While *asking* is important, *seeking* is also important. Seeking involves personal "efforts and labours" that can be used by God to address the very issues that brought the believer to his knees. If the prayer is to feed the hungry, should that not include personal effort to help provide for those in need? Though personal resources may be limited, they are not worthless. The notion that one's responsibility ends with a thoughtful prayer misses the point of Scripture concerning the believer's relationship with his/her fellowman. Perhaps the prayer should be a petition for God to provide additional resources so that person who is praying can have an even greater impact. It stands to reason, then, that a successful prayer life involves *seeking* as much as it involves *asking*.

When it comes to prayer – and particularly when it comes to petitioning God – certain matters are implied by the immediate text and by Scripture generally. For instance, the first thing to consider is whether or not the one praying has a proper spiritual relationship with him. If no such relationship with God exists, it seems unreasonable to expect him to listen to a prayer that comes out of the blue from one who has never sought him and does not walk with him. While it is true that a father will not give his son a stone when the son has asked for bread, it is probably fair to say that this same father may not be equally attentive to the request of a stranger. Therefore, one's spiritual standing must be considered. It is God's children who are positioned to approach him? Someone who is a stranger, spiritually speaking, is in no position to petition God and expect him to listen.

It is important to avoid using prayer as a tool to present God with a shopping list. If this is the primary motivation for prayer, it shows a lack of respect for the worth of prayer. In that case, it might be wise to revisit the Lord's Prayer on a regular basis to have a sense of what prayer is all about. Prayer is a spiritual tool that is intended to help an individual build a relationship with God. It is safe to say that a selfish prayer will not be viewed favorably by God.

Another matter to consider is whether a prayer aligns with God's will. For instance, people commonly pray for someone to live when they are deathly ill or injured, and there is certainly nothing wrong with that kind of prayer. Hezekiah prayed that God would extend his life and God did just that, allowing him an additional fifteen years (2 Kings 20: 1-7). At the same time, according to Scripture "...it is appointed for men to die once and after this *comes* judgment" (Hebrews 9: 27). Consequently, prayer cannot keep someone alive forever.

Scripture teaches that certain matters may require more than prayer. For instance, when the disciples could not cast out a demon, the text intimates, parenthetically, that this was not a matter of prayer only, but of prayer and fasting (Matthew 17: 14-21). It is difficult to say exactly what circumstances may rise to that level, but there may be times when God hopes that a prayer will be accompanied by a greater degree of solemnity. Therefore, it is in keeping with biblical principles to consider fasting on a regular basis, in complement with prayer, as a matter of Christian discipline.

Fasting, it seems, may be an example of what Ellicott had in mind when he wrote of *knocking at the gate with urgency*. Fasting extends one's faculties beyond mere asking in order to emphasize to God the greater concern in connection with a specific matter.

It is also important to leave the answering of prayers in God's hands, trusting that he is faithful. In the Lord's Prayer, Jesus stated, "...Your will be done" (Matthew 6: 10). The will of God must have the highest priority when it comes to prayer. Faith involves trusting that God's answer to a prayer is the best answer. As a matter of faith, the believer accepts that God knows best. He remains faithful even when a prayer is not answered as he had hoped.

In order to keep one's prayer life vital and avoid discouragement, it would be wise to refrain from anticipating how God should answer a prayerful petition. He does not think as people think, so allow God the freedom to answer as he sees fit. He has a much larger view of life and can take into consideration the bigger picture. His answers bear much better fruit.

Prayer serves as a lifeline to God. While bible study and corporate worship are not insignificant where one's spiritual well-being is concerned, it is undoubtedly the time spent in private that can make a person's relationship with God come alive. In one form or other (pray, prayed, prayer, praying), the word *pray* appears 362 times in God's Word. This is a good measure of the importance God places on personal communication with him. Ignoring a serious prayer life will, no doubt, prevent an individual from developing a meaningful walk with God.

The Golden Rule

Having addressed the matter of prayer and the benefits of a healthy prayer life, Jesus followed with a comment that is, as with certain other statements in this sermon, one of the more recognized verses of Scripture. Known by most as the golden rule, Jesus remarks, "In everything, therefore, treat people the same way you want them to treat you, for this is the Law and the Prophets" (v. 12).

The word "Therefore" (v. 12) indicates that Jesus' next words are directly related to the teaching in the preceding verses. It is a summary of the discussions on judging other people (vv. 1-6) and petitioning God, especially when those petitions concern others (vv. 7-12). The golden rule is an uncomplicated statement where Jesus has explained how believers should interact with others. One should judge others as he would want to be judged.

The compact yet profound character of these words is understood even by unbelievers. In fact, it is the innate wisdom found within these words that has surely caused them to be spoken somewhere in the world on a daily basis for the past two millennia and they will undoubtedly be repeated by someone every day until Jesus returns. Few teachings are quite so distinguished.

The Christian's treatment of people should reflect his relationship with God. In truth, a believer's treatment of others *will* replicate his/her relationship with God. Therefore, a believer who mistreats others may wish to examine the condition of that relationship. It has often been said that believers are the only Jesus unbelievers will see. That responsibility requires treating others in such a way that, when they see the attitude and actions of a faithful believer, they ultimately see Jesus. Godly people will respect others as God's creation and love them as he does.

How one is treated by others will most likely be a reflection of how that person acts toward others. Having no ill will with one's fellowman is beneficial in many ways. Life is certainly less stressful and that makes it much easier to live happily and with a measure of contentment. Therefore, the one who treats others respectfully generally ends up realizing the greatest benefits in relationships.

It stands to reason that Jesus' instruction on behavior toward others eclipses the mere notion of regarding them respectfully. He indicates that it is important to *do* for others and not merely *regard* them politely or avoid treating them poorly. The Greek *poieite* literally translates into *be doing*. The golden rule is not just about thought…it is about action. The ideas of surprising people with kindness or going the extra mile when it is not expected seem to fit well here. So, too, ministering to those who are hurting and helping those in need fit the bill. It is safe to say, then, that Jesus does not want believers to simply avoid treating others poorly. He wants those who call him Lord to be proactive in relationships, treating others *as they wish to be treated*. In doing so, those who receive *golden* treatment will more than likely reciprocate. That is the thoughtful wisdom of the golden rule.

Chapter Nine
Matthew 7: 13-20

The Narrow Gate

As he approached the end of his sermon, Jesus turned his attention to the very purpose of his presence on earth. He was here to provide a path to eternal life. He wanted the people to understand that spending eternity in heaven is no small feat. It is not easily realized. On the contrary, those who hope to attain eternal life and reach heaven will find that they must enter through what Jesus called the "narrow gate" (v. 13). This is complemented elsewhere in Scripture where Jesus himself stated that he is the only way to heaven (John 14: 6).

The path to destruction, on the other hand, is much easier to follow and takes little effort. Jesus stated that "…the gate is wide and the way is broad that leads to destruction" (v. 13). Indeed, all it takes is failure to believe (Mark 16: 16) for one to successfully navigate that particular path. It is relatively easy to deny Jesus, but it can be very challenging, as a matter of faith, to accept him as savior and live a life bathed in Christian discipleship. For this reason, few will follow the narrow path, and few will enter through the narrow gate that leads to life. Many will not enter the narrow gate simply because they are not looking for it. As a consequence, perhaps due to negligence or indifference, they will simply fail to recognize the path to life (v. 14), much less walk it.

False Teachings

One of the major difficulties when it comes to following the straight and narrow is *recognizing* the path to life. Conflicting messages concerning that path can make it difficult to identify. Some misconstrue the lessons of Scripture, leading themselves and others in a direction where "…the gate is wide and the way is broad" (v. 13).

Jesus, Peter, and Paul each offered dire warnings against misleading instruction.

"For false Christs and false prophets will arise and will show great signs and wonders, so as to mislead, if possible, even the elect." (Matthew 24: 24)

"But I am afraid that, as the serpent deceived Eve by his craftiness, your minds will be led astray from the simplicity and purity *of devotion* to Christ." (2 Corinthians 11: 3)

"Let no one deceive you with empty words, for because of these things the wrath of God comes upon the sons of disobedience." (Ephesians 5: 6)

"[3] If anyone advocates a different doctrine and does not agree with sound words, those of our Lord Jesus Christ, and with the doctrine conforming to godliness, [4] he is conceited *and* understands nothing; but he has a morbid interest in controversial questions and disputes about words, out of which arise envy, strife, abusive language, evil suspicions, [5] and constant friction between men of depraved mind and deprived of the truth, who suppose that godliness is a means of gain." (1 Timothy 6: 3-5)

[20] But know this first of all, that no prophecy of Scripture is *a matter* of one's own interpretation, [21] for no prophecy was ever made by an act of human will, but men moved by the Holy Spirit spoke from God. (2 Peter 1: 20-21)

…as also in all *his* letters, speaking in them of these things, in which are some things hard to understand, which the untaught and unstable distort, as *they do* also the rest of the Scriptures, to their own destruction. (2 Peter 3: 16)

These warnings against false teachings are severe. Jesus and the apostles were concerned that believers would be persuaded to blindly follow the path "…that leads to destruction" (v. 13). They were to hold fast to apostolic instruction, a message that permeates the New Testament. They were to teach the gospel message as they had received it.

Unfortunately, the deceitful nature of these false prophets might be difficult to recognize since, according to Jesus, they "…come to you in sheep's clothing, but inwardly are ravenous wolves" (v. 15). In other words, they may well appear to be godly men and women, but, in truth, they are deceivers set out to destroy God's kingdom.

How can one recognize those who seek to lead astray? According to Jesus, they are revealed by their fruit. Exactly what does he mean by fruit? Is he talking about the fruit of the Spirit? Is this a reference to their accomplishments?

It is probably fair to say that the fruit of which Jesus spoke is not the fruit of the spirit mentioned in Paul's letter to the Galatians. People can, to a certain degree, imitate true Christianity by being kind and patient. Additionally, Jesus' ensuing words suggest that he was more interested in their kingdom accomplishments, stating that "every good tree bears good fruit" (v. 17). However, it is not just their achievements by which they must be measured. Their works and teaching must be weighed against biblical instruction.

Twice Jesus stated "You will know them by their fruits" (vv. 16 & 20). This is true of those who deceive as well as those who teach the truth. Both are identified in the passage. Those who "...bear good fruit" (v. 17) are teachers of the truth. Those who "...bear bad fruit" (v. 17) are the *ravenous wolves* Jesus mentioned earlier (v. 15) and must be recognized as such. These will receive their just reward when they are "...cut down and thrown into the fire" (v. 19).

Jesus' lesson concerning false teachers was aimed at the general discipleship. While the spiritual gift of discernment was distributed to certain believers after the Day of Pentecost, Jesus suggested here that it was the responsibility of every believer to be on the lookout for false teachers. According to D. A. Carson:

Jesus does not explicitly say who will have the discernment to protect the community but implies that the community itself, by whatever agency, must somehow protect itself from the wolves.[20]

In the New Testament, the church elders are given the responsibility of shepherding the flock (1 Peter 5: 1-2). It stands to reason, then, that protection of the sheep against ravenous wolves would fall upon their shoulders. For this reason, it is imperative to have elders who know and teach biblical truth. Still, should an elder

---

[20] Carson, D. A., *The Expositors Bible Commentary with the New International Version, Matthew Chapters 1 through 12*, Zondervan Publishing House, Grand Rapids, 1995, p. 191.

begin teaching things contrary to Scripture, it is upon the members of the congregation to recognize the deviant teaching and avoid being deceived.

It can be difficult to identify false teachers for a variety of reasons, not the least of which is the fact that they may not even realize their teaching is false. Indeed, one who is teaching false doctrine may be entirely sincere, confident that he/she is teaching according to Scripture. However, sincerity is not the scale by which truth can be measured. For instance, the Baptist denomination insists that baptism is intended only for those who believe in Jesus as the Messiah and that said baptism must be by immersion in water. However, those of the Roman Catholic persuasion teach that even unaware infants may be baptized. They also believe that immersion is not necessary and that sprinkling water on an individual constitutes saving baptism.

On the surface these doctrines are obviously contradictory. Consequently, both cannot be true. Yet, there is every reason to believe that Baptists are completely genuine in their teaching concerning believer's baptism. Roman Catholics are equally sincere in their teaching. Since both teachings cannot be true, sincerity is not the scale by which truth can be measured.

Chapter Ten
Matthew 7: 21-29

Pseudo Disciples and the Day of Judgment

Jesus addressed the idea of *sincere* false teaching in the next few verses by presenting a scenario for his listeners to consider. He introduced the lesson with the statement, "Not everyone who says to Me, 'Lord, Lord,' will enter the kingdom of heaven, but he who does the will of My Father who is in heaven *will enter*" (v. 21). He then looked forward to *that day* (v. 22), which is, according to scholars, a reference to the Second Coming and the judgment. Indeed, the text itself suggests that Jesus had in view the final Day of Judgment. According to Jesus, on *that day* many will be disappointed when they appear before him in anxious anticipation of their heavenly reward. They will rely on their works (prophesying, casting out demons, performing miracles) as demonstration of their faithfulness and deservedness of their reward.

Unfortunately, they will not participate in eternal life in heaven as they had planned. The text reveals the reason they would be denied. Jesus will respond to them, "I never knew you; DEPART FROM ME, YOU WHO PRACTICE LAWLESSNESS" (v. 23). In addition, below are certain other English renderings of this verse that may be helpful.

Then I will tell them plainly, 'I never knew you. Away from me, you evildoers!' (NIV)

And then will I profess unto them, 'I never knew you: depart from me, ye that work iniquity.' (KJV)

Other translations are pretty much in keeping with the ones given here. What does it mean to *practice lawlessness* or *work iniquity*? What was Jesus suggesting with the term *evildoers*? The Greek word that is translated *iniquity*, or *lawlessness*, is *anomia*. The English word with which people are most familiar that accurately expresses the idea of *anomia* is *unrighteousness*. In other words, these people were guilty of *practicing unrighteousness*, or *being unrighteous* - the direct opposite of godliness.

Given the context of Jesus' words, it is not difficult to determine that his answer is juxtaposed against his comment regarding those who would enter the kingdom of heaven (v. 21). Evidently, these counterfeit disciples are among those who said "Lord, Lord" but did not do the will of the father. The text does not indicate precisely where they fell short, but it does reveal that their shortfall was serious enough to prevent their entrance into the eternal kingdom.

Nothing in this passage suggests that these people were insincere in their belief and their actions. They seem to believe they were earnestly serving the Lord. Their retort, as they highlighted what they considered their many kingdom successes (v. 22), indicates their astonishment that they would not receive an eternal reward. In fact, given their list of what they saw as righteous accomplishments, they probably believed they were among God's elite, making Jesus' answer even more shocking.

Jesus' remarks indicate that these people not only had no eternal heavenly reward awaiting them but, in actuality, they had never been part of the kingdom despite their apparent belief in Jesus (they were working in his name) or their belief that they were doing God's work. His words, "I never knew you..." (v. 23) make this clear. This is confirmed as Jesus offers a parable that further explains his lesson. He follows the story of these pseudo disciples with the word "Therefore" (v. 24). Thus, he purposefully links the story he had just told with the parable he was about to share, indicating that the intent behind the parable was to further explain why these souls were lost.

The Parable of the Builders

The parable of the builders confirms that the pseudo disciples Jesus mentioned were people who had not done the father's will. Jesus stated, "Therefore everyone who hears these words of Mine and acts on them, may be compared to a wise man who built his house on the rock" (v. 24). With this statement, Jesus was identifying them as those who had failed to act on his teachings.

Wise men build upon a foundation of rock while the unwise build on less stable foundations. That is the lesson of the well-known parable of the two builders. In this case, it is safe to say that those mentioned in Jesus' storyline had built on sand rather than rock. This explains Jesus' statement, "I never knew you..." (v. 23). The reason Jesus did not recognize them as his faithful is that they had never established a proper foundation upon which a relationship with him could be built. They were like the foolish builder who had built upon a foundation of sand, which is no foundation at all.

These last few verses (vv. 21-27), where Jesus talked about counterfeit disciples who would not receive an eternal reward and then provided an explanation via the parable of the builders, are prefaced by and grounded in Jesus' discussion of false teaching (vv. 13-20). Those who did not receive their eternal reward failed to do so because of false teaching. Similarly, false teaching is represented as a foundation of sand in the parable of the builders. In other words, whether someone advocates or is a follower who is simply deceived by it, false teaching can keep one from receiving an eternal heavenly reward.

The parable of the builders marks the end of the *Sermon on the Mount*, but the lessons would live on. Matthew notes that "...the crowds were amazed at His teaching; for He was teaching them as *one* having authority, and not as their scribes" (vv. 28-29). The Greek word translated as *teaching* (didache) could be a reference to Jesus' teaching style, the substance of his message, or both. In this case, it stands to reason that both are in view. Jesus could teach with spell-binding excellence and the long-lasting results reflect the substantive character of his words.

The character of Jesus' teaching (both style and substance) is compared to that of the scribes (v. 29). When Jesus spoke, he did so in a way that indicated that the teaching was his to offer. When a scribe taught, *'Thus sayeth the Lord'* would be repeated often. That is because the teaching must be accredited. However, Jesus was/is Lord. He had no need or reason to recognize another authority. His listeners seemed to appreciate that distinction.

Summary

The lessons in the *Sermon on the Mount* include some of the most profound and most godly teaching ever spoken. Jesus' words in this sermon provide foundational guidelines for how men ought to live their lives. Following these guiding principles not only leads to a life that benefits the individual and humanity in general, but it also serves to honor God.

The world sees life very differently than believers. Consequently, the words spoken by Jesus are foolishness to those who have no desire to serve or honor God. Selflessness, generosity, and showing little concern for wealth make no sense to the world. For the unbeliever, life is generally about self.

Jesus sought to change the human mindset through the words of his sermon. He hoped to help people focus more on their spiritual nature, which is undoubtedly why this sermon was recorded. This is an important read for any and all who seek to live wise, godly lives.

People often face seemingly insurmountable challenges. Jesus' sermon does not spell out the answer for each individual circumstance someone might face, but he does lay out principles that can help a person deal effectively with any situation. Therefore, returning to these words and re-reading this sermon on a consistent basis is arguably one of the wisest decisions an individual can make.

Bibliography

Arnold, Clinton E., Editor, *Zondervan Illustrated Bible Backgrounds Commentary, Volume 1*, Zondervan Publishing, Grand Rapids, MI, 2002

Bell, Brian, *Brian Bell Commentary on the Bible*, https://www.studylight.org/commentaries/cbb/matthew-5.html, Accessed March 20, 2017

Carson, D. A., *The Expositors Bible Commentary with the New International Version, Matthew Chapters 1 through 12*, Zondervan Publishing House, Grand Rapids, MI, 1995

Clarke, Adam, *The Adam Clarke Commentary*, http://classic.studylight.org/com/acc/view.cgi?book=mt&chapter=005, Accessed 01/15/2017

Clarke, Adam, *The Adam Clarke Commentary*, http://classic.studylight.org/com/acc/view.cgi?book=mt&chapter=006, Accessed 02/05/2017

Coffman, James B., *James Burton Coffman Commentaries – Matthew*, ACU Press, Abilene, TX, 1974

Coke, Thomas, *Thomas Coke Commentary on the Holy Bible*, https://www.studylight.org/commentaries/tcc/matthew-5.html, Accessed March 20, 2017.

Ellicott, Ellicott's *Commentary for English Readers*, https://www.studylight.org/commentaries/ebc/matthew-7.html, accessed 03/21/2017

Excel, Joseph S., Spence-Jones, Henry, editors, *Pulpit Commentary*, http://biblehub.com/commentaries/pulpit/matthew/5.htm, accessed March 3, 2017

Gill, John, *John Gill's Exposition of the Whole Bible*, https://www.studylight.org/commentaries/geb/matthew-5.html, Accessed March 6, 2017

Jamieson, Robert, Fausset, A. R., Brown, David, *Commentary Critical and Explanatory of the Whole Bible*, https://www.studylight.org/commentaries/jfb/matthew-7.html, Accessed April 4, 2017

Johnson, B. W., *the People's New Testament*, Gospel Light Publishing Co., Delight, AR.

McGarvey, J. W., *A Commentary on Matthew and Mark*, Gospel Light Publishing, Delight, AR.

Wenham, G. J., Mother, J. A. , Carson, D. A., and France, R. T., editors, *New Bible Commentary*, Intervarsity Press, Nottingham, England, 1994

GUARDIAN
PUBLISHING, LLC